BABY NAMES
For Boys

James L. Dalby

ISBN-13: 978-1480063778
ISBN-10: 1480063770

FOREWARD

Choosing a name for your baby is probably one of the most important decisions you can make in your child's life. It can affect his attitudes towards himself and others and how he perceives himself in relation to the rest of society. Choosing the wrong name for your child can leave him feeling like he doesn't belong or fit in.

Take into consideration what you would feel like if you grew up as Chester and was constantly called the common nickname 'Chester the molester.' There are a great number of names that lend themselves to taunting and teasing, simply because of the immaturity of other people. This can affect a child's self-esteem, or even leave him prone to being bullied for no reason.

Consider your ancestry. If you are of English descent, consider names of Kings like Edward or William. If you are of Russian decent, consider Czars like Nicolas or Ivan. Naming your baby based on your cultural heritage is a common method, and usually turns out pretty well, that is, unless you're of African descent and name your kid Shakazulu.

Have some common sense. Would you want to grow up with the name you are considering for your child? That should pretty much sum up the decision making process when you are choosing your baby's name.

It's your decision, but be open to other people's ideas. Sometimes a suggestion of a friend or family member hits the nail on the head. Also, be certain to take your spouse's opinion into consideration, because it's their child too. In fact, it is common to name a child after a family member such as your parent or grandparent.

In this list of 5000+ boys baby names, duplicates are kept to a minimum so that more names could be included in the list. This is by no means a complete list, but it has a wide variety of names from different origins, and have a diverse set of meanings. You'll be sure to come up with some good ideas from these suggestions.

BABY NAMES FOR BOYS

NAME	ORIGIN	MEANING
Aakarshan	Hindu	Attraction
Aaron	Hebrew	Exalted. Aaron was the brother of Moses in the Bible.
Abaddon	Hebrew	Destruction.
Abba	Hebrew	A father.
Abban	Latin	White.
Abbas	Arabic	Stern.
Abbott	Old English	Father of the abbey.
Abdel	Arabic	Servant
Abdiel	Hebrew	Faithful servant of God.
Abdieso	Persian	
Abdul	Arabic	The son of, or servant of.
Abdullah	Arabic	The servant of Allah.
Abe	Hebrew	Father of a multitude.
Abejundio	Spanish	Relating to the abaje (bee)
Abel	Hebrew	A breath. A son of Adam and Eve in the Bible.
Abelard	Teutonic	Nobly resolute.
Abenzio	Celtic	
Abercio	Latin	
Abernethy	Scottish Gaelic	The mouth of the Nethy River.
Abhay	Hindu	A son of Dharma.
Abhi	Hindu	
Abhijit	Hindu	A constellation dear to Hari.
Abhinav	Hindu	
Abhishek	Hindu	
Abhorson		From Shakespeare's play Measure for Measure.
Abi	Turkish	An elder brother.

Abie	Hebrew	Breath, or the son of Adam and Eve in the Bible. See Abel.
Abiel	Hebrew	God is the father.
Abijah	Hebrew	The Lord is my father.
Abir	Arabic/Hebrew	Arabic: The fragrant one. Hebrew: Strong.
Abisha	Hebrew	God's gift.
Abner	Hebrew	Father of light. A Biblical name.
Abraham	Hebrew	Father of a multitude.
Abram		High father.
Abrasha	Hebrew	Father.
Absalom	Arabic	The father of peace. A son of David in the Bible. See Axel.
Abudemio	Assyrian	
Abundiantus	Latin	Plentiful.
Acacio	Hebrew	The Lord holds.
Acario	Latin	Ungrateful.
Accursius	Latin	To hasten.
Ace	Latin	Unity.
Acelin	French	Noble.
Achilles	Greek	A handsome figure in Greek mythology.
Achyuta	Hindu	A name of Vishnu.
Ackerley	Old English	A dweller in the meadow.
Ackley	Old English	A dweller in the Oak tree meadow.
Acton	Old English	From the settlement with Oak trees.
Acuzio	Latin	Sharp.
Adair	Scottish Gaelic	From the Oak tree near the ford.
Adalardo	Celtic	Noble.
Adalgiso	Old German	Noble hostage.
Adalrico	Latin, Old German	Noble, powerful and rich.
Adam	Hebrew	A man of the red earth. According to the Bible, the first man.
Adar	Hebrew	Fire.
Addai	Hebrew	Man of God.
Addison	Old English	Son of Adam. A man of the red earth.

Addo	Teutonic, Hebrew	Happy, ornament.
Adeben	Ghanese	Twelfth-born son.
Adeipho	Greek	A brother.
Adel	Teutonic	Noble.
Adelais	Latin	Noble.
Adelard	Teutonic	Nobly resolute.
Adelbert	Old German	Famous for nobility.
Adelfried	Old German	Who protects the descendants.
Adelino	Old German	Noble.
Adelmo	Old German	Noble protector.
Adelphos	Greek	Brother.
Ademaro	Old German	Glorious in battle.
Aden	Arabic	Fiery one.
Adeodatus	Latin	Given by God.
Adhamh	Irish/Scottish	A man of the red earth. According to the Bible, the first man.
Adin	Hebrew	Sensual.
Adir	Hebrew	Noble, majestic.
Adiran	Latin	Of the Adriatic.
Aditya	Hindu	Lord of the sun.
Adlai	Hebrew	My witness. A Biblical name.
Adler	Teutonic	An eagle. A man of keen perception.
Adley	Hebrew	Just.
Admes	Greek	
Admon	Hebrew	Red peony.
Adnan	Arabic	The settler.
Adney	Old English	A dweller on the island.
Adolfo		Wolf.
Adolph	Teutonic	Wolf.
Adon	Hebrew	The Lord.
Adoni	Aboriginal	The sunset.
Adonis	Greek	In mythology, the handsome youth loved by Venus.
Adony	Hungarian	
Adrastos	Greek	Undaunted.

Adrian	Latin	Dark, rich.
Adriel	Hebrew	From God's congregation.
Aegeon		From Shakespeare's play Comedy of Errors.
Aemilius		From Shakespeare's play Titus Andronicus.
Aeneas	Greek	The praised one.
Aeolus	Greek	In mythology, the ruler of the winds.
Aeron	Welsh	An unusual boy's name.
Aetos	Greek	Eagle.
Afro	Latin	From Africa.
Agabo	Hebrew	
Agamemnon		From Shakespeare's play Troilus & Cressida.
Agatone	Greek	Good, kind.
Agilard	Teutonic	Bright.
Agosto	Italian	Venerable, the exalted one.
Agrippa		From Shakespeare's play Antony & Cleopatra.
Agu	Nigerian	A leopard.
Agustin	Spanish	Venerable, the exalted one.
Ahab	Hebrew	An uncle. A king of Israel in the Bible.
Ahearn	Irish Gaelic	A horse-keeper, or a steward.
Ahmed	Arabic	Most highly praised.
Ahmik	Hebrew	Strength of God's flock.
Ahren	Teutonic	An eagle.
Aidan	Irish Gaelic	The little fiery one.
Aiken	Old English	Little Adam.
Ailen	Old English	Made of oak.
Aimery	Teutonic	Industrious ruler.
Aimon	French from Teutonic	A house.
Aindreas	Scottish	Scottish Gaelic form of Andrew. Manly, courageous.
Ainsley	Old English/Scottish	A meadow or clearing. Also a unisex name.
Aitan	Hebrew, African	Fights of possession.

Ajani	Nigerian	The victor.
Ajatashatru	Hindu	A name of Vishnu.
Ajax	Greek	The legendary hero of the Trojan War.
Ajayi	Yoruban, Nigerian	Born face-down.
Ajit	Hindu	
Ajitabh	Hindu	
Akaash	Hindu	Sky.
Akama	Aboriginal	A whale.
Akando	Native American	Ambush.
Akbar	Arabic	Great.
Akello	Ugandan	I have bought.
Akil	Arabic	Intelligent.
Akim	Russian	Russian form of Joachim. Established by God.
Akira	Japanese	Intelligent.
Akiva	Hebrew	The supplanter.
Akiyama	Japanese	The autumn, and mountain.
Akram	Arabic	Generous, noble.
Aksel	Norwegian	The father of peace. A form of Absalom.
Akshay	Hindu	Name of a god.
Al	Irish and Scottish Gaelic	Handsome.
Aladdin	Arabic	A servant of Allah.
Alan	Irish and Scottish Gaelic	Handsome.
Aland	English	bright as the sun
Alarbus		From Shakespeare's play Titus Andronicus.
Alard	Teutonic	A noble ruler.
Alaric	Teutonic	The ruler of all.
Alasdair	Scottish	Protector of men.
Alastair	Scottish	Protector of men.
Alban	Latin	Fair complexioned. A saint's name.
Alber	Teutonic	A quick mind.

Alberich	Teutonic	The king of the dwarfs in German legend.
Albern	Old English	A noble warrior.
Albert	Teutonic	Noble, bright.
Albin	Latin	Fair complexioned. A saint's name.
Albion	Latin	White. Also an old name for England.
Alcander	Greek	Strong.
Alcibiades		From Shakespeare's play Timon of Athens.
Alcott	Old English	From the stone cottage.
Alden	Old English	An old, wise friend.
Alder	Old English	The Alder tree.
Alderney	English	One of the Channel Isles.
Aldous	Teutonic	Old, wise or great.
Aldred	Old English	A great counselor.
Aldrich	Old English	An old, wise ruler.
Aldridge	Old English	From the Alder tree ridge.
Aldwin	Old English	An old, wise friend.
Aldwyn	Old English	An old, wise friend.
Alec	Greek	The protector and helper of mankind. Also see Sanders.
Aled	Welsh	Offspring.
Alejandro	Spanish	The protector and helper of mankind. Also see Sanders.
Aleron	Latin	An eagle.
Aleser	Arabic	Lion.
Alessandro	Italian	The protector and helper of mankind. Also see Sanders.
Alex		The defender, or helper of mankind. A form of Alexander, but also used as an independent name.
Alexander	Greek	Protector of men.
Alexas		From Shakespeare's play Antony & Cleopatra.
Alexis	Greek	The protector and helper of mankind. A boy or girl's name.

Alfons	German	Noble and ready.
Alfonso	Teutonic	Noble and ready.
Alford	Old English	From the old ford.
Alfred	Old English	Counselor
Alger	Old English	A noble spearman.
Algernon	French	With whiskers, bearded.
Algren	unknown	
Ali	Arabic	Exalted, or noble. A boy or girl's name.
Alika	Polynesian	The defender of mankind.
Alim	Arabic	Wise, learned.
Alison	Old English	The light of the sun. A boy or girl's name.
Alistair	Scottish	The protector and helper of mankind. Also see Sanders.
Alister	Greek	The protector and helper of mankind. Also see Sanders.
Allambee	Aboriginal	A quiet resting-place.
Allan	Irish and Scottish Gaelic	Harmony, or the cheerful handsome one.
Allard	Old English	Sacred, brave.
Allen	Irish and Scottish Gaelic	Handsome.
Alleyne	Irish and Scottish Gaelic	Harmony, or the cheerful handsome one.
Allighiero	Italian	A noble spear.
Allister	Scottish	The protector and helper of mankind. Also see Sanders.
Almo	Old English	Noble and famous.
Almon	Hebrew	Forsaken.
Alok	Hindu	
Alonso	Spanish	Noble and ready.
Aloysius	Teutonic	A famous warrior.
Alphonse	Old German	Noble estate, eager.
Alphonso	Teutonic	Noble and ready.
Alric	German	A ruler.

Alroy	Irish Gaelic	A redheaded boy.
Alston	Old English	From the old place.
Altair	Arabic, Greek	Bird, star
Altman	Teutonic	An old wise man.
Alun	Welsh	Harmony, or the cheerful handsome one.
Alvah	Hebrew	The exalted one.
Alvin	Teutonic	Noble friend.
Alvis	Old Norse	All wise.
Alwan	Teutonic	A noble friend.
Alwin	Teutonic	Beloved by all.
Alwyn	Teutonic	A noble friend.
Amadeus	Latin	Love of God.
Amadi	Nigerian	General rejoicing, seemed destined to die.
Amado	Latin	Loving deity.
Amador	Spanish	Lover.
Amal	Arabic/Hebrew	Arabic: Hope. Hebrew: Work or labor.
Amar	Hindu	Forever.
Amaro	Portuguese	Dark, like a Moor.
Amaroo	Aboriginal	A beautiful place.
Amato	Spanish	Beloved.
Ambar	Sanskrit	Of the sky. A boy or girl's name.
Ambert	Teutonic	A bright, shining light.
Ambler	Old English	A stable-keeper.
Ambrose	Greek	Immortal.
Amery	Teutonic	Divine, or a famous ruler.
Amherst	English	Name of a location.
Amida	Japanese	The name of a Buddha.
Amiel	Hebrew	The Lord of my people.
Amiens		From Shakespeare's play As You Like It.
Amin	Arabic/Hebrew	Honest and trustworthy.
Amir	Arabic	Princely.
Amiri	Maori	The east wind.

Amirov	Hebrew	My people are great.
Amistad	Spanish	Friendship.
Amit	Hindu	Endless.
Amitabh	Hindu	
Amitava	Hindu	
Ammon	Egyptian	Hidden. The name of an ancient god.
Amol	Hindu	
Amon	Hebrew	Trustworthy.
Amory	Teutonic	Divine, or a famous ruler.
Amos	Hebrew	The bearer of burdens. The name of an Old Testament prophet.
Amrit	Sanskrit	The immortal one.
Amsden	Old English	From the valley of Ambrose.
Amul	Hindu	
Amulya	Hindu	Priceless.
Amund	Scandinavian	Divine protection.
Anand	Sanskrit	Joyful.
Anant	Hindu	
Anastasius	Greek	Resurrection, one who shall rise again.
Anatole	Greek	From the east.
Anay	Hindu	
Ancel	Teutonic	Godlike.
Anders	Scandinavian	Scandinavian form of Andrew. Manly, courageous.
Anderson	unknown	Son of Andrew
Andreus	Greek	Son of Peneius River.
Andrew	Greek	Manly, courageous.
Androcles	Greek	A man, and glory. A figure from Roman legend.
Aneurin	Welsh	Truly golden.
Ang	Swedish	
Angada	Hindu	A son of Lakshmana.
Angelo	Italian	An angel or saintly messenger.
Angus	Scottish Gaelic	Unique strength, outstanding.
Angwyn	Welsh	Very handsome.

Anieli	Greek	Manly.
Anil	Sanskrit	Of the wind.
Anirudhh	Hindu	
Anish	Hindu	
Aniston		
Anjuman	Hindu	A party place (mehfil).
Anker	Greek	Manly.
Ankit	Hindu	
Ankur	Hindu	
Annan	Celtic	From the stream.
Anniruddha	Hindu	Son of Pradyummna.
Anno	Hebrew	Grace. The masculine form of Anne.
Anoke	Native American	The actor.
Anoki	Native American	An actor.
Anoop	Hindu	Incomparable, the best.
Ansari	Arabic	A helper.
Anscom	Old English	A dweller in the secret valley.
Ansel	Old French	A nobleman's follower.
Anselm	Teutonic	A divine helmet. The name of a saint.
Anshul	Hindu	
Anshuman	Hindu	
Ansley	Old English	From the hermitage clearing.
Anson	Old English	The son of Anne or Agnes.
Anstice	Russian from Greek	The resurrected one. A boy or girl's name.
Antal	Latin	Prince.
Anthony	Latin	Worthy of praise.
Antigonus		From Shakespeare's play Winter's Tale.
Antiochus		From Shakespeare's play Pericles.
Antipholus		From Shakespeare's play Comedy of Errors.
Anton	German	Worthy of praise.
Antoni	Polish	Worthy of praise.
Antonio	Italian/Spanish	Worthy of praise.

Anu		The king of the gods in Babylonian mythology.
Anwar	Arabic	The bright one.
Anwell	Celtic	The beloved, dear one.
Anyon	Celtic	An anvil.
Apache		The name of a North American Indian tribe.
Apari	Aboriginal	Father.
Apemantus		From Shakespeare's play Timon of Athens.
Apollo	Greek	A beautiful youth. The God of music, poetry and healing in Greek mythology.
Apostolos	Greek	
Aquila	Latin	Like an eagle.
Ara	Armenian/Latin	Armenian: Kingly. Latin: An altar.
Araluen	Aboriginal	The place of waterlilies. A boy or girl's name.
Aram	Assyrian	high place
Aran	Hebrew	Active, nimble.
Arana	Polynesian	Polynesian form of Alan. Handsome.
Archard	Teutonic	Sacred and powerful.
Archer	Old English	A bowman.
Archibald	Teutonic	Very bold.
Archidamus		From Shakespeare's play A Winter's Tale.
Archie		Very bold.
Arden	Old English/Latin	Old English: A dwelling place. Latin: Ardent and sincere. A boy or girl's name.
Ardley	Old English	From the meadow of the home-lover.
Ardolph	Old English	The wolf (a wanderer) who longs for home.
Ardon	Hebrew	Bronze.
Aren	Nigerian	Eagle.
Arend	Dutch	Dutch form of Arnold.
Ares	Greek	God of war.

Name	Origin	Meaning
Argus	Greek	Watchful. A giant with a hundred eyes in Greek mythology.
Argyll	Scottish Gaelic	From the land of the Gaels. Also the name of a Scottish county.
Ari	Hebrew	A Lion.
Aric	Old English	A sacred ruler.
Aricin	Norwegian	the eternal kings son
Ariel	Hebrew	A lion of God.
Ariki	Polynesian	A chief.
Arion		A figure from Greek mythology.
Aristedes	Greek	Descended from the best.
Aristo	Greek	Best
Aristotle	Greek	A thinker. The name of a famous Greek philosopher.
Arizona		The name of a State in the USA.
Arje	Dutch	Dutch form of Adrian.
Arjun	Sanskrit	The white one.
Arkin	Norwegian	the eternal king's son
Arkwright	Old English	A carpenter.
Arland	Celtic	Pledge.
Arlen	Irish Gaelic	A pledge.
Arley	Old English	From the hare or stag meadow.
Arlo	Old English	From the protected town or hill.
Armand	French	Of the army.
Armande	French	Of the army.
Armando	Italian/Spanish	Of the army.
Armen	Armenian/Hebrew	Armenian: A man from Armenia. Hebrew: A castle.
Armon	Hebrew	Castle.
Armstrong	Old English	A strong-armed warrior.
Arnall	Teutonic	A gracious eagle.
Arnaud		Ruler of eagles.
Arne	Dutch	Eagle. Dutch form of Arnold.
Arnett	French	A little eagle.
Arnie		Eagle.

Arnold	Teutonic	Strong as an eagle. A name introduced to England by the Normans.
Arnon	Hebrew	Rushing stream.
Aron	Hebrew	Exalted.
Aronne	German/Italian	Exalted.
Aroon	Thai	Of the dawn.
Arpiar	Armenian	Sunny.
Arran	Scottish	The name of a Scottish island. A boy or girl's name.
Arsen	Greek	Strong
Arsenio	Greek	Manly, virile
Art	Celtic	A rock.
Arthur	Celtic	A follower of Thor and strong as a bear.
Arthus	Welsh	Bear hero, a rock.
Artie	Celtic	A follower of Thor.
Arty		A follower of Thor.
Aruiragus		From Shakespeare's play Cymbeline.
Arun	Sanskrit	The dawn.
Arundel	Old English	He who dwells with the eagles.
Arunta	Aboriginal	A white cockatoo.
Arvad	Hebrew	The wanderer.
Arval	Latin	From the cultivated land.
Arvin	Teutonic	A friend of the people.
Arvind	Hindu	
Arviragus		From Shakespeare's play Cymbeline.
Arwin	German	Uncertain, possibly friend of the army. Also see Erwin.
Asa	Hebrew/Japansese	Hebrew: The healer, a physician. A Biblical name. Japanese: The morning. A boy or girl's name.
Ascot	Old English	One who lives in the East cottage.
Aseem	Hindu	
Ash		Blessed, happy.
Ashburn	Old English	From the brook by the Ash tree.
Ashby	Old English	A farm by the Ash tree.

Asher	Hebrew	Blessed, happy.
Ashford	Old English	One who lives at the ford by the Ash tree.
Ashish	Hindu	Blessings.
Ashliegh	Old English	From the Ash tree.
Ashlin	Old English	A dweller by the Ash tree pool.
Ashok	Sanskrit	Without sadness.
Ashon	Ghanese	Seventh-born son.
Ashraf	Arabic	Honorable.
Ashton	Old English	One who lives at the Ash tree farm.
Ashur	Hebrew	Black.
Ashutosh	Hindu	
Ashwin	Hindu	Strong horse.
Ashwini	Hindu	
Asija	Hindu	A great sage, brother of Brihaspati.
Asim	Arabic	The protector.
Askel	Norse	A divine cauldron.
Aslak	Norse	Divine sport.
Asparouh	Bulgarian	Paro, Pouro.
Astin	unknown	Strong Leader, trustworthy.
Aston	Old English	From the Eastern place.
Asuman	Hindu	Lord of vital breaths.
Asvathama	Hindu	Son of Drona.
Asvin	Hindu	(Nasatya and Dasra) gods of medicine.
Aswad	Arabic	Black.
Aswin	Old English	A spear comrade or protector.
Asztrik	Hungarian	Made from ashenwood.
Atalik	Hungarian	Like his father.
Atarah	Hebrew	A crown. A boy or girl's name.
Atawn	Welsh	Harmony. Can be used as a form of Alan.
Athan	Greek	Immortal
Atharvan	Hindu	Knower of the Arthara vedas.
Athelstan	Old English	A noble stone. The name of an early English king.

Atherol	Old English	Dweller at the spring farm.
Atherton	Old English	One who lives at the spring farm.
Athol	Scottish Gaelic	New Ireland. A location.
Athos	Greek	An alternative name for Zeus, the ruler of the heavens.
Atilla	Hungarian	Beloved father.
Atiu	Polynesian	The eldest.
Atlas	Greek	A mythological demigod who supported the sky on his shoulders.
Atley	Old English	From the meadow.
Atmajyoti	Hindu	Light of Atma.
Atman	Hindu	The self.
Atrayl	Tray	
Atrus	Atrius	
Attila		The war-like king of the Huns.
Attis	Greek	Handsome boy.
Atul	Hindu	
Atulya	Hindu	
Atwater	Old English	One who hides by the water.
Atwell	Old English	A dweller by the spring.
Atworth	Old English	From the farm.
Auberon	Teutonic	Noble.
Aubert	French	Noble and illustrious.
Aubin	French	Fair complexioned. A saint's name.
Aubrey	Teutonic	The golden-haired ruler of the elves.
Auburn	Latin	Fair
Audric	French	An old, wise ruler.
Audun	Norwegian	Deserted.
Augustine	Latin	Belonging to Augustus. Venerable, the exalted one.
Augustus	Latin	Venerable, the exalted one. The name of the first great roman emperor.
Aurek	Polish	Golden-haired.
Aurelio	Latin	Gold.
Aurelius	Latin	The golden one.
Austell		The name of a Cornish Saint.

Austen		Modern form of Augustine. Venerable, the exalted one.
Austin		Modern form of Augustine. Venerable, the exalted one.
Autolucus		From Shakespeare's play A Winter's Tale.
Avan	Hebrew	Proud.
Avel	Greek/Hebrew/Russian	Breath. A boy or girl's name.
Avenall	Old French	A dweller in the Oat field.
Averell	Old English	The slayer of the boar.
Averill	Old English	boar-warrior
Avery	Old English	The ruler of the elves. A boy or girl's name.
Avinash	Hindu	
Aviv	Hebrew	Of the Spring (season).
Avner	Hebrew	The father of light. A Biblical name.
Avon	English	The name of an English county, and rivers in England and New Zealand.
Avram	Greek	The father of many.
Avrom	Hebrew	The father of many.
Axel	Teutonic from Hebrew	Source of all life.
Axton	Old English	The stone of the sword wielder.
Ayer	Old French	An heir.
Ayhner	Old English	Noble and famous.
Aylward	Old English	An awe-inspiring guardian.
Aylwin	Teutonic	A noble friend.
Ayush	Hindu	
Azariah	Hebrew	He whom the Lord helps.
Azi	Nigerian	A youth.
Azim	Arabic	Grand.
Aziz	Arabic	The powerful one.
Azriel	Hebrew	An angel of the Lord.
Azzan	Hebrew	Very strong.
Babar	Turkish	A Lion.

Babul	Hindu	
Bacchus	Greek	The Roman God of wine.
Bae	Korean	Inspiration.
Bahar	Persian	Baharak.
Bailey	Old French	A bailiff or administrative official.
Baingana	Swahili	People are equal.
Baird	Scottish Gaelic	A bard or minstrel.
Bairn	Scottish	Child.
Bajnok	Hungarian	Victor.
Bakari	Swahili	Promising.
Baker		
Balavan	Hindu	Powerful.
Balbo	Latin	Inarticulate.
Balder	Swedish	God of light.
Baldric	Teutonic	A bold or princely ruler.
Baldwin	Teutonic	A brave friend or protector.
Bale	Ugandan	Home of the Mutima clan.
Balfour	Scottish Gaelic	From the village by the pasture.
Bali	Hindu	Mighty warrior.
Balint	Latin	Strong and healthy.
Ballard	Teutonic	Strong, bold.
Balram	Hindu	
Balthasar	Greek	The Lord protects the king. One of the three wise men in the Bible.
Balthazar	Greek	The Lord protects the king. One of the three wise men in the Bible.
Balun	Aboriginal	A river.
Bancroft	Old English	From the bean field.
Bandele	Yoruban	Born away from home.
Bane	Hawaiian	Long-awaited child.
Banjora	Aboriginal	A Koala.
Bankim	Hindu	
Banning	Gaelic	Blond child.
Banquo		From Shakespeare's play MacBeth.
Bansi	Hindu	

Baptista	Latin	The baptized one.
Barabas	Hebrew	Barabba. The prisoner released by Pilot instead of Jesus.
Barak	Hebrew	A flash of lightning.
Baran	Latin	Form of star Aldebaran.
Barber	Latin	Beard
Barclay	Old English	From the meadow of the Birch tree.
Barden	Old English	From the valley of barley.
Bardo	Aboriginal	Water.
Bardolph		From Shakespeare's play Merry Wives of Windsor and Henry V
Bardon	Anglo-Saxon	Barley valley.
Barega	Aboriginal	The wind.
Barend	Dutch	A firm bear.
Bari	French, Celtic, Welsh	spear thrower, son of Harry, marksman
Barlow	Old English	From the barley hill.
Barna	Aramic	Son of comforting.
Barnabas	Hebrew	Son of a prophecy.
Barnard	Teutonic	As brave as a bear.
Barnardine		From Shakespeare's play A Winter's Tale.
Barnardo	Teutonic	Bold as a bear.
Barnet	Old English	From the place cleared by burning.
Barnett	Old English	Noble man.
Barney		As brave as a bear.
Barnum	Old English	A stone house.
Barny		As brave as a bear.
Baron	Old French	A nobleman.
Barrett	Teutonic	Bear-like.
Barry	Irish Gaelic	Like a spear.
Bars	Hungarian	Pepper.
Barse	English	Fresh-water perch.
Bart	Hebrew	Hill, furrow. From the name Bartholomew.

Barth	Hebrew	Hill, furrow. From the name Bartholomew.
Bartholomew	Hebrew	Hill, furrow.
Barton	Old English	From the Barley fields.
Baruch	Hebrew	Blessed.
Barwon	Aboriginal	A wide river.
Bashir	Arabic	A good omen.
Basil	Greek	Like a king.
Basim	Arabic	The smiling one.
Bassanio		From Shakespeare's play Merchant of Venice.
Bassett		From Shakespeare's play King Henry VI.
Bastiaan	Greek	venerable
Bastian	Latin	A man from Sebasta. The name of a 3rd-century saint.
Bastien	Latin	A man from Sebasta. The name of a 3rd-century saint.
Bates	unknown	A common last name.
Baudouin	French	A brave friend or protector.
Baul	English	Snail.
Bavol	English	Wind.
Baxter	Old English	A baker.
Bay	Vietnamese	Born on a Saturday. Also a herb and a reddish-brown color.
Bayanai	Filipino	Hero.
Bayard	Old French	With reddish-brown hair.
Bayley	Old French	A bailiff or administrative official.
Bazyli	Polish	Royalty
Beacan	Celtic, Gaelic	Small, little one.
Beacher	Old English	dweller by the beech tree
Beagan	Irish Gaelic	The little one.
Beaman	Old English	Beekeeper.
Beardsley	Old English	Beard, wood.
Beathan	Scottish Gaelic	Scottish Gaelic form of Benjamin. Son of my right hand.

Beattie	Irish Gaelic	The provider.
Beau	French	Handsome or beautiful. A boy or girl's name.
Beaumont	Old French	A beautiful hill or mountain.
Beauregard	Old French	Beautiful, handsome.
Bebe	French	Baby.
Becan	Irish Gaelic	A little one.
Beck	Old English	A brook or small stream.
Becse	Hungarian	The kite.
Bede	Old English	A prayer.
Bedrich	Czech	A peaceful ruler.
Bela	Hungarian	The white one. A boy or girl's name.
Belarius		From Shakespeare's play Cymbeline.
Beldon	Old English	Beautiful pasture, child of the unspoiled glen.
Belen	Greek	An arrow.
Bellamy	Old French	A handsome friend.
Bem	Nigerian	Peace.
Bemus	Greek	Platform.
Ben	Hebrew	Son of my right hand.
Bence	Hungarian	Victor.
Benedick	Latin	Son of my right hand.
Benedict	Latin	Son of my right hand.
Benito	Latin	Blessed.
Benjamin	Hebrew	A son of the south, or the son of the right hand. The brother of Joseph in the Bible.
Benjy		Son of my right hand.
Bennet	Latin	Little blessed one.
Bennett	Latin	Little blessed one.
Benny		Son of my right hand.
Benson	Old English	Son of Benjamin. Son of my right hand.
Bentley	Old English	From the bent grass clearing or meadow.
Benton	Old English	From the bent grass farm.

Benvolio		From Shakespeare's play Romeo & Juliet.
Berenger	French	Courage of a bear.
Berg	Teutonic	A mountain.
Bergen		The name of a Norwegian port.
Berger	Teutonic	From the mountains.
Bergren	Swedish	Mountain stream.
Beriszl	Hungarian	Honor.
Berk	Turkish	Solid and firm.
Berkeley	Old English	From the Birch tree wood or meadow.
Berkly	Old English	From the Birch tree wood or meadow.
Bernard	Teutonic	Bold as a bear.
Bernardo		From Shakespeare's play Hamlet.
Bernie		Bold as a bear.
Berny		Bold as a bear.
Berowne		From Shakespeare's play Love's Labour's Lost.
Berrigan	Aboriginal	Wattle.
Bersh	English	One year.
Bert		Bright, nobility.
Berthold	Teutonic	Glorious ruler.
Bertie		Bright, nobility.
Bertram	Teutonic	A bright raven.
Berwyn	Welsh	Fair-haired, or a bright friend. A boy or girl's name.
Besnik	Albanian	
Beval	English	Like the wind.
Bevan	Welsh	Son of Evan Young, warrior.
Beverly	Old English	From the stream of the beaver. A boy or girl's name.
Bevis	French	After the city of Beauvais, meaning a beautiful outlook or view.
Beyers		
Bhagirath	Hindu	

Bharat	Sanskrit	Being maintained. The name of the Hindu god of fire.
Bhaskar	Hindu	
Bhavesh	Hindu	
Bhavin	Hindu	Swedish
Bhavya	Hindu	
Bhim	Hindu	
Bhima	Sanskrit	The mighty one.
Bhishma	Hindu	
Bhrigu	Hindu	A Prajapati.
Bhudev	Hindu	Lord of the Earth.
Bhupen	Hindu	
Bhupendra	Hindu	
Bhuvan	Hindu	
Bialy	Polish	White-haired boy.
Bilal	Arabic	First convert of Muhammad.
Bill		A strong and resolute protector.
Billy		A strong and resolute protector.
Bing	Old English	From the hollow.
Bingham	Old English	Crib.
Binyamin	Jewish	A son of the south, or the son of the right hand. The brother of Joseph in the Bible.
Biondello		From Shakespeare's play Taming of the Shrew.
Birch	Old English	At the Birch tree.
Bishop	Old English	A bishop.
Bitalo	Uganda	Finger-licking.
Bjorn	Old Norse	Like a bear. Also see Bernard.
Blade	Old English	Glory, prosperity.
Blaine	Irish Gaelic	Thin. A boy or girl's name.
Blair	Scottish Gaelic	From the plain or field. A boy or girl's name.
Blaise	Latin	One who lisps or stammers. A boy or girl's name.
Blake	Old English	Fair-haired. A boy or girl's name.

Blakeley	Old English	From the black meadow.
Blaxland	Old English	From the black land.
Blaxton	Old English	A black stone.
Blaz	Old German	Unwavering protector.
Bledig	Welsh	Like a wolf.
Blythe	Old English	Joyous and cheerful. A boy or girl's name.
Bo	Old Norse/Chinese	Old Norse: A householder. Chinese: Precious. A boy or girl's name.
Boa		
Boaz	Hebrew	Swift and strong. The husband of Ruth in the Bible.
Bob	Teutonic	Famous, bright fame. Also see Hopkin, Robert, Robertson and Robinson.
Bobbie	Teutonic	Famous, bright fame. A boy or girl's name.
Bobby	Teutonic	Famous, bright fame. A boy or girl's name.
Bod	Hungarian	Branch.
Boden	Old French	Herald.
Bodo	Teutonic	A leader.
Bodor	Hungarian	Curly.
Bogart	Old French/Teutonic	A strong bow.
Bogdan	Slavonic	A gift from God.
Bolton	Old English	Of the manor farm.
Bonamy	French	A good friend.
Bonar	Old French	Kind and gentle.
Bond	Old English/Old Norse	A peasant farmer.
Bonner	Old French	Gracious, gentle.
Booker	Old English	Beech tree.
Boone	Latin, French	Good
Booth	Old Norse	A shelter.
Borachio		From Shakespeare's play Much Ado About Nothing.

Borden	Old English	From the valley of the boar.
Borg	Scandinavian	From the castle.
Boris	Slavonic/Russian	Warrior.
Bosley	Old English	A grove of trees.
Boswell	Old French	Forested town.
Bosworth	Old English	From the boar enclosure.
Botan	Japanese	Peony.
Botond	Hungarian	Mace wielding warrior.
Bottom		From Shakespeare's play Midsummer-Night's Dream.
Boult	Cornish	From Shakespeare's play Pericles.
Bourke	Old English	From the fort or hill.
Bowen	Welsh	Son of Owen.
Bowie	Scottish Gaelic	Golden-haired.
Bowman	English	the archer
Boyce	Old French	From the wood, or forest.
Boyd	Scottish Gaelic	Yellow-hair.
Boyden	Anglo-Saxon	A herald.
Boyet		From Shakespeare's play Love's Labour's Lost.
Brabantio		From Shakespeare's play Othello.
Brad		Broad meadow.
Braden	Old English	From the wide valley.
Bradford	Old English	A broad ford.
Bradley	Old English	A broad lea, meadow.
Bradwell	Old English	From the broad stream.
Brady	Irish Gaelic	From an old surname.
Brae	Cornish/Gaelic	A hill.
Brahnan	courageous one	Brahn, Brahni.
Bram	Hebrew	The father of many.
Bramwell	English	A location.
Bran	Celtic	A raven.
Branch	Latin	Extension.
Brand	Swedish	Sword blade.
Brandeis	German	Dweller on a burned clearing.

Brander	Old Norse	A fiery sword.
Brandon	Old English	A raven.
Branko	Slowenian	
Brant	Teutonic	Firebrand.
Braxton		Brock's town.
Bray	Old English	To cry out.
Brayden		Brave.
Braz	Latin	Stammerer.
Brazil		The name of a South American country.
Brecon	Welsh	The name of a group of mountains.
Brencis	Latin	Crowned with laurel.
Brendan	Irish Gaelic	A raven.
Brennan		Raven-like.
Brent	Old English/Celtic	A steep climb.
Breok	Cornish/Welsh	The name of an early saint.
Breton	Old English	From a location in Somerset.
Brett	Old English	Briton, British.
Brewster	Middle English	One who brews beer.
Briac	Celtic	Esteem.
Brian	Celtic	Strong one.
Briand	French	Castle.
Brice	Celtic	The son of Rice.
Brigham	Old English	Covered bridge.
Brighton	Hebrew	The one who is loved.
Brij	Hindu	
Brijesh	Hindu	
Brinley	Old English	Tawny.
Brishen	English	Born during a rain.
Bristol	unknown	
Brock	Old English	A badger.
Broderick	Welsh	Son of Roderick. A renowned ruler.
Brodie	Irish Gaelic	A ditch. A boy or girl's name.
Brodny	Slavic	One who lives near a shallow stream crossing.

Brody	Welsh	Son of Roderick. A renowned ruler.
Brom	Gaelic	Raven.
Bromley	Old English	From the place where broom grows.
Bronson	Old English	Strong, fierce one.
Brook	Old English	At the brook or stream. A boy or girl's name.
Brooke	Old English	At the brook or stream. A boy or girl's name.
Broughton	Old English	From the town on a hill.
Brown	Middle English	A color.
Bruce	Old French	Woods.
Bruno	Teutonic	Brown haired.
Brutus	Latin	Broodish.
Bryan		Strong one.
Bryant		Strong, honorable
Bryce	Celtic	The speckled, or freckled, one.
Brychan	Welsh	The speckled, or freckled, one.
Bryn	Welsh	A hill. A boy or girl's name.
Brynmor	Welsh	A large hill.
Buck	Old English	A lover of horses.
Buckley	Old English	From the meadow of the buck deer.
Bud	American	Messenger, friend. Originally a short form of buddy (friend), but now used as an independent name, particularly in the USA.
Buddy		Friend.
Budi	Indonesian	The wise one.
Burchard	Teutonic	A strong protector.
Burdon	Old English	A dweller at the hill fort.
Burgess	Old French from Teutonic	The citizen of a town.
Burhan	Arabic	Proof.
Burian	Ukranian	He lives near the weeds.
Burke	Old English	From the fortress.
Burl	Old English	A cup bearer or wine server.
Burle	Middle English	Knotted wood.

Burley	Old English	From the fort or castle meadow.
Burnaby	Old Norse	The warrior's estate.
Burnard	Teutonic	As brave as a bear. Also see Bjorn.
Burne	Old English	Brook.
Burnell	Old French	The little brown-haired one.
Burnet	Old French	The brown one. Also a plant name.
Burnu	Aboriginal	A tree.
Burnum	Aboriginal	A great warrior.
Burr	Swedish	Youth.
Burt	English	A short form of the name Burton. Also a variation of Bert.
Burton	Old English	From the fortified farm or town.
Busby	Old Norse	From the farm in the thicket.
Buster	English	A nickname, but it is sometimes used independently.
Butler	Old French	The head servant.
Byford	Old English	A dweller by the ford.
Bylent	Turkish	
Byng	Old English	From the hollow.
Byron	Old English	Bear or cottage.
Cable	Old French	Rope.
Cadby	Old Norse	The warrior's settlement.
Cadell	Welsh	The battle spirit.
Cadeo	Vietnamese	Folk song.
Cadman	Celtic	A man of battle.
Cadmus	Greek	A man from the east. A mythological figure.
Cadogan	Old Welsh	Honor in battle.
Caedmon	Celtic	A wise warrior.
Caerwyn	Welsh	A blessed or holy fort.
Caesar	Latin	The name of the famous Roman emperor.
Cahil	Turkish	Young and inexperienced.
Cailan	Gaelic	Child.
Cailean	Scottish Gaelic	The victory of the people.

Cain	Hebrew/Old French	The son of Adam and Eve who murdered his brother Abel. Old French: Battlefield. Also see Cane.
Caine		The son of Adam and Eve who murdered his brother Abel. Old French: Battlefield. Also see Cane.
Caithness		From Shakespeare's play Macbeth.
Caius		From Shakespeare's play Titus Andronicus.
Cajan		
Cal	Old English	A calf herder.
Calder	Old English	Stream.
Caldwell	Old English	Cold spring.
Caleb	Hebrew	The devoted one.
Caley	Irish Gaelic	Slender. A boy or girl's name.
Calhoun		Warrior.
Caliban		From Shakespeare's play The Tempest.
Calisto	Greek	Most beautiful.
Calixto	Latin	A chalice.
Callis	Latin	Cup.
Calum	Scottish	Dove.
Calvert	Old English	A calf herder.
Calvin	Latin	The little bald one.
Calvine		The little bald one.
Cam	Vietnamese, English	Orange fruit, sweet, beloved, referring to the sun.
Camden	Gaelic	From the winding valley.
Cameron	Scottish Gaelic	A crooked nose. From an old Scottish surname.
Camille	Latin	Virginal, unblemished character. Also from a Roman family name. A boy or girl's name.
Camillo		From Shakespeare's play Winter's Tale.
Camlin	Celtic	Crooked line.

Campbell	Scottish Gaelic	A crooked mouth. The name of one of the great Scottish highland clans.
Candan	Turkish	Sincerely.
Candidius		From Shakespeare's play Antony & Cleopatra.
Cane	Gaelic	An old surname.
Canice	Irish Gaelic	The handsome one. The name of several early saints.
Cannon	Kannon, Canon	
Canute	Old Norse	A knot. The name of several Danish kings.
Capers		
Caphis		From Shakespeare's play Timon of Athens.
Capucius		From Shakespeare's play Henry VIII.
Capulet		From Shakespeare's play Romeo & Juliet.
Caradoc	Celtic/Welsh	Beloved or amiable.
Carden	Celtic	from the black fortress
Cardew	Cornish/Welsh	The black fort.
Carel	Dutch	A free man.
Carey	Irish/Celtic/Cornish	Irish: The name of a castle. Celtic: From the river. Cornish: The loved one. A boy or girl's name.
Carl	German	A free man.
Carleton		Carl's town or farmer's town.
Carlin	Cornish/IrishGaelic	Cornish: From the fort by the pool. Irish Gaelic: The little champion. A boy or girl's name.
Carlisle	Old English	The location of the fort.
Carlo	Italian	A free man.
Carlos	Portuguese/Spanish	A free man.
Carlton	Old English	From the settlement of the free peasants.
Carlyle	Old English	Carl's island.
Carlyon	Cornish	From the slate earthworks.

Carmelo	Hebrew	From the garden. After mount Carmel in the holy land.
Carne	Cornish	A pile of rocks.
Carnelian		The name of a gemstone. A boy or girl's name.
Carr	Old Norse	From the marshland. Also see Carson.
Carrick	Irish Gaelic	A rocky cliff or cape.
Carrington	Old English	Beautiful.
Carroll	Irish Gaelic	A fierce warrior.
Carson	Old English	From the marshland. Son of Carr.
Carsten	German	A follower of Christ. A Christian.
Carsyn		From the marshland. Son of Carr.
Carter	Old English	A cart driver or maker.
Carvell	Old French	The marshy estate, or the estate of the spear man
Carver	Old English	Wood carver.
Carwyn	Welsh	Blessed love.
Cary	Irish/Celtic/Cornish	Irish: The name of a castle. Celtic: From the river. Cornish: The loved one. A boy or girl's name.
Case	Old French	Chest.
Casey	Irish Gaelic	The vigilant one. A boy or girl's name.
Casimir	Old Slavonic	The great destroyer.
Caspar	Persian	The treasurer. The name of one of the three wise men in the new testament. Also see Gaspar and Jasper.
Casper	Persian	Treasurer.
Cassidy	Irish Gaelic	The clever or ingenious one.
Cassio		From Shakespeare's play Othello.
Cassius	Latin	Vain.
Castel	Spanish	Belonging to a castle.
Cathal	Irish Gaelic	A battle ruler.
Cathan	Irish Gaelic	Of the battle. Also see Kane.
Cathmor	Irish Gaelic	A great warrior.
Cato	Latin	The wise one.
Caton	Spanish	Knowledgeable, wise.

Cavan	Irish Gaelic	The handsome one.
Cayden	Gaelic	Spirit of battle.
Ceasar	Latin	To cut.
Cecil	Latin	The blind one.
Cedric	English	Chief. Invented in the early 1800's by Sir Walter Scott for a character in Ivanhoe.
Cemal	Arabic	Perfect.
Cengis	Turkish	
Cerimon		From Shakespeare's play Pericles.
Cesar	French	The name of the famous Roman emperor.
Chad	Old English	Battle, warrior. From the name of a 7th-century saint.
Chadwick	Old English	Battle, warrior.
Chahaya	Indonesian	Light.
Chaika	Hebrew	Life.
Chaim	Hebrew	Life.
Chal	English	Boy, son, male.
Chale	Spanish	Strong and manly, masculine
Challis	Old French	A ladder or stairs.
Chalmers	Scottish	Son of the Lord
Chaman	Hindu	
Chan	Chinese	A Chinese clan name.
Chance	Old French	A church official or chancellor. A boy or girl's name.
Chancellor		Keeper of records, secretary.
Chancey	Old French	A church official or chancellor.
Chandan	Sanskrit	Of the Sandalwood tree.
Chander	Cesar, Cezar	
Chandler	Old French	Candle maker.
Chandra	Sanskrit	A shining moon. A boy or girl's name.
Chane	Hindu, Swahili	Name of a god, dependability.
Chaney	Old French	From the Oak grove.
Channing	Old French	A canon.
Chapal	Hindu	

Chapin	Old French	Clergyman.
Chapman	Old English	A merchant or trader.
Charan	Hindu	
Charles	Teutonic	Manly, full grown.
Charleton	Old English	From the settlement of the free peasants.
Charlton	Old English	From the settlement of the free peasants.
Chas	Teutonic	Manly, full grown.
Chase	Old French	The hunter.
Chata	African	An ending.
Chatillon		From Shakespeare's play King John.
Chaucer	Old French	A boot maker.
Chauncey	Old French	A church official or chancellor.
Chayton	Sioux	Falcon.
Chen	Chinese	Great or vast.
Cheney	Old French	From the Oak grove.
Cherokee	Native American	The name of a tribe.
Chester	Latin	A Roman site or camp. Also the name of an English city.
Chet	Thai	A brother.
Chetan	Hindu	
Chetwin	Old English	From the cottage on the winding path.
Chevalier	French, Old English	Knight, chase, hunt.
Chevy	French	From chevalier, meaning knight.
Cheyenne	Native American	A tribe. Also a city in the USA.
Cheyney	Old French	From the Oak grove.
Chiamaka	African	God is splendid
Chico	Teutonic	A free man.
Chike	African	Power of god.
Chilton	Old English	From the children's farm.
Chin	Korean	The precious one.
Chinmay	Hindu	
Chintu	Hindu	
Chiranjeev	Hindu	

Chiron	Greek	A wise teacher.
Chrirag	Hindu	
Chris		Bearing Christ. The patron saint of travelers. Also see Christian.
Christian	Latin	A follower of Christ. A Christian. A boy or girl's name.
Christie	Irish/Scottish	A follower of Christ, a Christian. A boy or girl's name.
Christmas	Old English	Born at Christmas time. A boy or girl's name.
Christopher	Greek	Bearing Christ. The patron saint of travelers Also see Christian.
Christos	Greek	Christ.
Christy	Irish/Scottish	A follower of Christ, a Christian. A boy or girl's name.
Chrysander	Greek	A golden man.
Chuck	Teutonic	Manly, full grown.
Chuckie	Teutonic	A free man.
Chung	Chinese	The wise one.
Churchill	Old English	From the church on the hill.
Cian	Irish Gaelic	Ancient. Also see Keane.
Ciaran	Irish	Dark, black.
Cicero	Latin	Historian. Also the name of a famous Roman statesman and orator.
Ciceron	Latin	Chickpea.
Ciel	French	From heaven.
Ciprian	Latin	A man from the island of Cyprus.
Ciprien	French	A man from the island of Cyprus.
Ciro	Italian	The name of the founder of the Persian empire. From the name Cyrus.
Clachas		From Shakespeare's play Troilus & Cressida
Clancy	Irish Gaelic	A red or ruddy warrior.
Clarence	Latin	Clear, luminous.
Clark	Old French	A cleric or scholar. Also see Cleary.
Clarke		A cleric or scholar. Also see Cleary.

Claude	Latin	The lame one.
Claudio	Italian/Spanish	The lame one.
Claudius	German	The lame one.
Claus	Dutch/German	The victory of the people.
Clay	Old English	From the clay.
Clayland		From the clay.
Clayton	Old English	Town on clay land.
Cleary	Irish Gaelic	A clerk or scholar. Also see Clark.
Cledwyn	Welsh	Rough but blessed.
Clem		Gentle, merciful.
Clemens		Gentle, merciful. From the name Clement.
Clement	Latin	Gentle, merciful.
Cleon	Greek	The famous one.
Cleve	Old English	From the hilly place, or the place of cliffs.
Cleveland	Old English	Land of high cliffs.
Cliff		From the ford by the cliff or slope.
Clifford	Old English	From the ford by the cliff or slope.
Clifton	Old English	From a town near a cliff.
Clint		The place on the headland.
Clinton	Old English	The place on the headland.
Clitus		From Shakespeare's play Julius Caesar.
Clive	Old English	Cliff.
Cloten		From Shakespeare's play Cymbeline.
Clovis	Teutonic	A famous warrior.
Clunes	Scottish Gaelic	A resting-place, or meadow.
Clyde	Scottish	The name of a river.
Coalan	Celtic	Slender.
Cobar	Aboriginal	Burnt earth.
Cobden	Old English	From the hill with a knob.
Cobweb		From Shakespeare's play Midsummer-Night's Dream.
Cody	Old English	A pillow or cushion. A boy or girl's name.

Cohn	Greek	The victory of the people.
Colbert	Teutonic	A bright seafarer.
Colby	Old Norse	From the dark country.
Cole	Old English/Teutonic	Dark and swarthy.
Coleman	Teutonic/Latin	Teutonic: Dark. Latin: Like a dove. Also see Calum and Columba.
Colin		Fire. Also see Cohn.
Collin		Fire. Also see Cohn.
Colman		Little dove.
Colon	Spanish	Dove.
Coltin	Colt, Kolt	
Colton	Old English	From the dark town.
Columba	Latin	Dove-like. The name of a 6th-century Irish saint. Also see Calum and Coleman. A boy or girl's name.
Coman	Arabic	Noble.
Comfort	Latin	Strengthen.
Cominius		From Shakespeare's play Coriolanus.
Compton	Old English	From the farm in the valley.
Conall	Celtic	As strong as a wolf.
Conan	Irish Gaelic	Wise and intelligent.
Condon	Celtic	The dark-haired wise man.
Conlan	Irish Gaelic	The hero.
Conley		Hero.
Conn	Irish Gaelic	A chief. Also used as a diminutive of Connor.
Conner		Wise.
Connley		Hero.
Connor	Irish Gaelic	A strong will.
Conor		A strong will.
Conrad	Teutonic	Bold, wise counselor From the name Conrad and Curtis.
Conrade		From Shakespeare's play Much Ado About Nothing.
Conroy	Irish Gaelic	Wise.
Constantine	Latin	Firm, constant.

Conway	Welsh/Irish	Welsh: Holy water. Irish: A yellow hound.
Cooper	Middle English	Barrel maker.
Coorain	Aboriginal	The wind. Also a location in New South Wales.
Corban	Greek	A gift devoted to God.
Corbett	Old French	A raven.
Corcoran	Gaelic	Of reddish complexion.
Cordell	Old French	A rope maker.
Corey	Celtic/Gaelic	Dweller in the hollow. A boy or girl's name.
Corin	Cornish/Latin	Cornish: From the corner. Latin: The name of a Roman deity, possibly meaning a spear. Also from Shakespeare's play As You Like It. A boy or girl's name.
Cormac	Irish Gaelic	The lad of the chariot.
Cornelian		The name of a gemstone. A boy or girl's name.
Cornelius	Latin	Horn-colored
Cornell		Horn-colored
Cort	Old German	Bold.
Corwin	Old French	A friend of the heart.
Cory		Helmet. A boy or girl's name.
Cosmo	Greek	Perfect order, harmony.
Costard		From Shakespeare's play Love's Labour's Lost.
Coty	English	old house
Court		From Shakespeare's play Henry V.
Courtland	Old English	From the court land.
Courtney	Old French	The short-nosed one, or a location. A boy or girl's name.
Craig	Scottish Gaelic	A rock or crag.
Crandon	Old English	From the hill of the cranes.
Cranley	Old English	From the meadow of the cranes.
Cranmer		From Shakespeare's play Henry VIII.
Cranog	Welsh	A heron.

Name	Origin	Meaning
Crawford	Old English	From the ford with the crows.
Creighton		Near the creek.
Crewe	Old English	Stepping stones or a ford. An English location.
Crisiant	Welsh	Like a crystal. A boy or girl's name.
Crispin	Latin	Curly-haired. St. Crispin was a 3rd-century martyr.
Cristian	Latin	A follower of Christ. A Christian.
Cristiano	Italian	A follower of Christ. A Christian.
Cristo	Spanish	Bearing Christ. From the name Christopher.
Cromwell	Old English	From the winding stream.
Cronan	Irish Gaelic	The swarthy one.
Crosby	Old Norse	From the village with the cross.
Csaba	Hungarian	From mythology, shepherd, wanderer.
Cseke	Hungarian	Puller, carrier.
Csenger	Hungarian	
Csepel	Hungarian	Young forest.
Csombor	Hungarian	
Csongor	Hungarian	Hunting bird.
Ctirad	Czech	
Cuba		The name of a Caribbean country.
Cubert	Cornish	A Celtic saint and a location.
Cullen	Old French	Handsome.
Cupid	Latin	Desire, passion. The ancient Roman god of love, and son of Venus.
Curan		From Shakespeare's play King Lear.
Curio		From Shakespeare's play Twelfth Night.
Curnow	Cornish	From Cornwall.
Curran	Irish Gaelic	An old family name.
Currier	Old English	Churn.
Curry		A marsh or a spice.
Curt	Teutonic	Bold, wise counselor From the name Conrad and Curtis.
Curtis	Old French	Courteous.

Cuthbert	Old English	Brilliant.
Cutler		Knife maker.
Cutter		Gem cutter.
Cy	Persian	The name of the founder of the Persian empire. From the name Cyrus.
Cymbeline		From Shakespeare's play Cymbeline.
Cynfor	Welsh	A great chief.
Cynric	Old English	Of kingly lineage.
Cyprian	Latin	A man from the island of Cyprus.
Cyrano	Greek	A man from Cyrent an ancient Greek colony in North Africa.
Cyric	Celtic	
Cyril	Greek	Lordly.
Cyrus	Persian	The name of the founder of the Persian empire.
Dabert	French	Bright action.
Dacey	Gaelic	The southerner. A boy or girl's name.
Dade	unknown	
Dafydd	Welsh	Beloved.
Dag	Old Norse	The day.
Dagan	Hebrew	Grain, or the earth.
Dagobert	German	Shining sun.
Dahana	Hindu	A Rudra.
Dai	Welsh/Japanese	Welsh: The beloved, the adored one. Japanese: Great. A boy or girl's name.
Dail	Teutonic/Old English	A valley dweller. A boy or girl's name.
Dakarai	African	Happiness.
Dakota	Native American	A friend.
Dakshesh	Hindu	
Daku	Aboriginal	Sand.
Dalbert	Old English	From the shining valley.
Daley	Irish Gaelic	A counselor.
Dallas	Celtic	Skilled, or from the field of water. Also a city in Texas. A boy or girl's name.
Dallin	Old English	Pride's people.

Dalton	Old English	The town near the valley.
Daly	Gaelic	Advisor.
Dalziel	Scottish Gaelic	From the little field.
Damek	Czech	Earth.
Damen	Greek	Taming
Damian	Greek	Tame, domesticated. Also a true friend.
Damien	Greek	Tame, domesticated. Also a true friend.
Damodar	Sanskrit	Tied with a rope around the belly.
Damon	Greek	Day or constant.
Dan	Hebrew	God is my judge. An Old Testament prophet.
Dana	Old English/Czech	Old English: From Denmark. Czech: God is my judge. A boy or girl's name.
Danby	Old Norse	From the Dane's settlement.
Dane	Old English	From Denmark. A boy or girl's name.
Daniel	Hebrew	God is my judge. An Old Testament prophet.
Danior	English	Born with teeth.
Dannie	Hebrew	God is my judge.
Danny	Hebrew	God is my judge.
Dante	Italian	Enduring, steadfast. Also see Durant.
Dara	Irish Gaelic/Hebrew	Irish: A son of oak. Hebrew: Compassion, wisdom. A boy or girl's name.
Darby	Irish Gaelic/Middle English	Irish Gaelic: Free from envy. Middle English: The deer settlement. A boy or girl's name.
Darcy	Old French	Dark. Also from a location and a Norman family name.
Darel	Aboriginal	Blue sky.
Daren	Nigerian	Born at night. Also see Darren.
Darien	Greek/Spanish	Greek: Wealthy. Spanish: A location.
Darin		Precious present.
Darius	Greek	Wealthy. The name of several ancient Persian kings.

Darnell	French	From the hidden place.
Darrel	Old English	Beloved.
Darrell	Old French	The dear one, the beloved.
Darren	English	Great.
Darryl		Dear, beloved.
Darshan	Hindu	A god's name.
Dartagnan	French	Leader.
Darthmouth	English	Port's name.
Darton	Old English	From the deer forest or estate.
Daruka	Hindu	
Darwin	Old English	A beloved friend.
Daryl		Dear, beloved.
Dattatreya	Hindu	A son of Atri, a god.
Dave		Beloved. From the name David, but also used independently.
Davey	Hebrew	The beloved, the adored one. From the name David.
David	Hebrew	The beloved, the adored one. The famous Israelite king of the Bible, and the patron saint of Wales. Also see Davidson.
Davidson	English	The beloved, the adored one.
Davie		The beloved, the adored one. From the name David.
Davin	Scandinavian	The bright one from Finland.
Davis	Scottish	David's son
Davy		The beloved, the adored one. From the name David.
Dawa	Tibetan/Sherpa	Born on a Monday. A boy or girl's name.
Dayton		Bright and sunny town.
Deacon	Greek	Servant, messenger.
Dean	Latin/Old English	Latin: A soldier. Teutonic: Merciful.
Decker	Belgian	Roofer.
Declan	Irish Gaelic	The name of a 5th-century bishop.

Decretas		From Shakespeare's play Antony & Cleopatra.
Dedric	Teutonic	A ruler of the people. Also see Theodoric.
Dedrick	German	A ruler of the people. Also see Theodoric.
Deepak	Sanskrit	Like a lamp or light.
Deiphobus		From Shakespeare's play Troilus & Cressida.
Del	Teutonic	A ruler of the people. From the name Derek and names beginning with 'Del'.
Delaney	Gaelic	The challenger's descendant.
Delano	Old French	From the forest of nut trees.
Delbert	Old English	Bright as day.
Deli	Hungarian	Warrior.
Dell	English	From the dell or hollow. A boy or girl's name.
Delling	Old Norse	The shining one.
Delmar	Latin	From the sea.
Delmore	Latin	Sea.
Delroy	Old French	The son or servant of the king.
Delsin	Native American	He is so.
Delwyn	Old English/Welsh	Old English: A friend from the valley. Welsh: Neat and fair. A boy or girl's name.
Deman	Dutch	Man.
Demas	Greek	Popular.
Demetrius	Greek	Goddess of fertility.
Demitrius		Lover of the earth.
Demos	Greek	Of the people.
Dempe	unknown	Peace
Dempsey	Irish Gaelic	The proud one.
Dempster	Old English	The judge.
Demyan	Russian	Tame, domesticated. Also a true friend.
Denby	Old Norse	From the Dane's settlement.

Denes	Greek, Hungarian	Wine, drama.
Denham	Old English	A homestead in the valley.
Denholm	Swedish	Home of the Danes.
Denis		Wild, frenzied. Also a lover of wine. From Dionysus, the mythological God of wine and drama. Also see Dennison and Tennyson.
Deniz	Turkish	Of the sea.
Denley	Old English	From the meadow in the valley.
Dennis	Greek	Wild, frenzied. Also a lover of wine. From Dionysus, the mythological God of wine and drama. Also see Dennison and Tennyson.
Dennison	Old English	The son of Dennis. Wild, frenzied. Also a lover of wine. Also see Tennyson.
Denton	Old English	From the farm or town in the valley.
Denver	Old English	From the edge of the valley. Also an USA city.
Denzel	Cornish	From a location meaning high stronghold.
Denzil	Cornish	From a location meaning high stronghold.
Deo	Greek	Godlike.
Derain	Aboriginal	Of the mountains.
Derby	Irish Gaelic/Middle English	Irish Gaelic: Free from envy. Middle English: The deer settlement.
Derek	Teutonic	A ruler of the people. Also see Theodoric.
Derex		A ruler of the people. Also see Theodoric.
Dermot	Irish Gaelic	Envy free.
Derrell	Old French	The dear one, the beloved.
Derren		From an old Welsh name.
Derrick	Cornish	From the Oak grove. Also see Derek.
Derron		Great.

Derry	Cornish/Irish Gaelic	Cornish: Of the Oak trees. Irish Gaelic: Redheaded, and the name of an Irish county. Also see Derek.
Derward	Old English	The deer-keeper.
Derwent	Welsh	The name of rivers in England and Tasmania.
Derwin	Old English	A beloved friend.
Derwood	Old English	The gatekeeper.
Derwyn	Old English	A beloved friend.
Des		Short for names beginning with Des.
Desiderio	Latin, French	Long hoped for, craved, desired.
Desiderius	Latin	The desired one.
Desmond	Irish Gaelic	The world.
Dev	Sanskrit	Godlike.
Devang	Hindu	
Devante	Spanish	Fighter of wrong.
Devarsi	Hindu	Sage of the Devas
Devdan	Sanskrit	The gift of the gods.
Deverell	Celtic	From the riverbank.
Devereux	Old French/English	Originally a Norman surname.
Devesh	Hindu	
Devi	Breton/Sanskrit	Breton: The beloved, the adored one. Sanskrit: Godlike, a goddess. A boy or girl's name.
Devin	Celtic	A poet.
Devitri	Hindu	
Devlin	Irish Gaelic	Fierce bravery.
Devon	English	The name of a Southwestern English county.
Devrity	Hindu	
Dewey	Welsh	Devin
Dewi	Welsh	Welsh form of David. The beloved, the adored one. Also see Dafydd.
Dewitt	Welsh	blond
Dexter	Latin	Right-handed, dexterous.
Dhananjay	Hindu	Arjuna

Dharma	Hindu	
Dharmavira	Hindu	
Dharmendra	Hindu	
Dharmesh	Hindu	
Dharuna	Hindu	A rishi.
Dhatri	Hindu	A son of Vishnu, Lakshmi
Dhaval	Hindu	
Dheran	Aboriginal	A gully.
Dhruv	Hindu	
Diamond	Old English	A shining protector.
Dian	Indonesian	A candle.
Diarmad	Scottish Gaelic	Without envy.
Diarmid	Irish Gaelic	Without envy.
Dick	Teutonic	Powerful, rich ruler.
Dickie	Teutonic	Brave and strong.
Dickinson	Old English	Powerful, a rich ruler.
Dickson	Old English	The son of Richard (Dick's son). Brave and strong.
Dicky	Teutonic	Brave and strong.
Didier	French	The desired one.
Diederik	Danish	ruler of the people
Diego	Spanish	Spanish form of James. The supplanter. Also see Santiago.
Dieter	Old German	Of a warrior race.
Dietrich	German	A ruler of the people. Also see Theodoric.
Digby	Old Norse	From the settlement by the dyke.
Diggory	Cornish from Old French	Lost or strayed.
Dilip	Hindu	A king, ancestor of Rama.
Dillon	Welsh	Man from the sea.
Dimitri	Greek	Belonging to Demeter, the `Earth Mother' and goddess of fertility.
Dinesh	Sanskrit	The lord of the day.
Dinkar	Hindu	

Name	Origin	Meaning
Dino	Italian	Latin: A religious official. Old English: From the valley.
Dinsdale	Welsh	Born on Sunday.
Diomedes		From Shakespeare's play Antony & Cleopatra, Troilus & Cressida.
Dion	Greek	A lover of wine. From Dionysus, the mythological God of wine and drama. Also see Dennison and Tennyson.
Dione	Greek	A lover of wine. From Dionysus, the mythological God of wine and drama. A boy or girl's name.
Dionysus	German	A lover of wine. From Dionysus, the mythological God of wine and drama. Also see Dennison and Tennyson.
Dirk	Dutch/Flemish	A ruler of the people. Also see Theodoric.
Dirke	Teutonic	A ruler of the people. Also see Theodoric.
Divyesh	Hindu	
Dixon	Old English	Richard's son.
Djavan	Brazilian	
Dmitri	Greek	Goddess of fertility.
Dobry	Polish	Good.
Dodd	Teutonic	Of the people.
Dogberry		From Shakespeare's play Much Ado About Nothing.
Dolabella		From Shakespeare's play Antony & Cleopatra.
Dolan	Irish Gaelic	Black-haired.
Dolf	Teutonic	A noble wolf.
Dolph	Teutonic	A noble wolf.
Dominic	Latin	Belonging to the Lord. St Dominic founded an important order of monks.
Dominick		Belonging to God.
Domokos	Hungarian	God's own.
Don	Scottish Gaelic	The ruler of the world. From the name Donald and other `Don' names.

Donahue	Irish Gaelic	A warrior dressed in brown.
Donalbain		From Shakespeare's play MacBeth.
Donald	Scottish Gaelic	The ruler of the world.
Donatien	French, Latin	Gift.
Donato	Latin	A gift, given by God.
Donegal	Irish	The name of a county.
Donnelly	Gaelic	The dark brave one.
Donnie	Scottish Gaelic	The ruler of the world. From the name Donald and other `Don' names.
Donny	Scottish Gaelic	The ruler of the world. From the name Donald and other `Don' names.
Donoghue	Irish Gaelic	A warrior dressed in brown.
Donohue	Irish Gaelic	A warrior dressed in brown.
Donovan	Irish Gaelic	Dark warrior.
Dooley	Irish Gaelic	A dark hero.
Dorak	Aboriginal	Lively.
Doran	Irish Gaelic	A wanderer or stranger.
Dorian	Greek	A man belonging to the Dorian tribe (one of the ancient Greek tribes). Oscar Wilde probably invented the name for the main character of his 1890s novel, The Portrait of Dorian Gray.
Dorjee	Tibetan/Sherpa	A thunderbolt.
Doron	Greek	A gift. A modern Jewish name, and the masculine form of Dora.
Dorset	Old English	Tribe near the sea.
Dory	French	Golden-haired.
Doug		From the dark stream.
Dougal	Gaelic	A dark stranger.
Douglas	Scottish Gaelic	From the dark stream.
Douglass		From the dark stream.
Dov	Hebrew	A bear.
Dover	Old English	Of the waters.
Dow	Irish Gaelic	Black-haired.
Doyle	Gaelic	A dark stranger.

Dragan	Slavonic	The dear one.
Drake	Old English	Dragon.
Drew	Celtic	Courageous. A boy or girl's name.
Driscoll	Irish	The interpreter.
Dromio		From Shakespeare's play Comedy of Errors.
Drostan	Celtic	The noisy one.
Druce	Celtic	The son of Drew. Manly, courageous. From the name Andrew, but also an independent name.
Drury	Old French	The dear one, a sweetheart.
Dryden	Old English	From the dry valley.
Drystan	Celtic	The noisy one.
Duane	Irish Gaelic	A little dark one.
Duarte	Portuguese	Portuguese form of Edward. Happy guardian.
Dudley	English	From the meadow.
Duff	Scottish Gaelic	Dark-haired, or of a dark complexion.
Dugal	Gaelic	A dark stranger.
Dugald	Gaelic	A dark stranger.
Dugan	Gaelic	Dark-skinned.
Duglas	Gaelic	dark stranger
Duke	Old French	Leader.
Dull		From Shakespeare's play Love's Labour's Lost.
Dumaine		From Shakespeare's play Love's Labour's Lost.
Duman	Turkish	Smoke, or mist.
Dunbar	Gaelic	A dark branch.
Duncan	Scottish Gaelic	Dark skinned warrior.
Dunham	Celtic	A dark man.
Dunley	Old English	From the meadow of the Roe deer.
Dunmore	Scottish Gaelic	From the fortress on the hill.
Dunn	Celtic	Brown.
Dunstan	Old English	From the dark stone or hill.
Dural	Aboriginal	A hollow tree that is on fire.

Durand	Latin	Enduring.
Duranjaya	Hindu	A heroic son.
Durant	Latin	Enduring, steadfast. Also see Dante.
Durdanius		From Shakespeare's play Julius Caesar.
Durham	Old English	A hilly peninsula.
Durjaya	Hindu	Hard to conquer.
Durmada	Hindu	
Durriken	English	Fortune-telling. Intuitive.
Durward	Old English	The gatekeeper.
Durwin	Old English	A dear friend.
Dusan	Czech	The soul, the spirit.
Dustin	Old Norse	Warrior.
Dutch	German	The German.
Dvimidha	Hindu	
Dwaine	Irish Gaelic	A little dark one.
Dwane	Irish Gaelic	A little dark one.
Dwayne	Irish Gaelic	A little dark one.
Dwennon	Old English	One of originality.
Dwight	Teutonic	White, fair one.
Dyami	Native American	An eagle.
Dyfan	Welsh	Welsh form of Damon. Day or constant.
Dylan	Welsh	Man from the sea.
Dymas	Greek	Father of Hecate.
Dyre	Scandinavian	A dear or precious one.
Eachan	Scottish Gaelic	A brown horse.
Eamnonn	Irish Gaelic	Irish Gaelic form of Edmund. Protector.
Eamon		Protector.
Earl	Old English	A nobleman.
Earnest	Teutonic	The serious, earnest one.
Earvin	Scottish	From a location (Irving).
Eaton	Old English	From the estate by the river.
Eban	Hebrew	Stone.

Ebenezer	Hebrew	The rock of help. A location that is mentioned in the Bible.
Eberhard	Teutonic	As brave as a wild boar. Also see Everard.
Ebrahim	Arabic	Arabic form of Abraham.
Ed	Old English	Happy guardian. From the name Edgar, Edmund, Edward, Edwin and other names.
Edan	Irish Gaelic	The little fiery one.
Edbert	Old English	Prosperous and bright.
Eddie		Great spearman.
Eddy		Great spearman.
Eden	Hebrew/Old English	Hebrew: The place of pleasure (from the Garden of Eden). Old English: A bear cub. A boy or girl's name.
Edgar	Old English	Great spearman.
Edgardo	Old English/French	prosperous warrior
Edison	Old English	The son of Edgar, Edmund or Edward. Great spearman.
Edlin	Old English	A prosperous friend.
Edmond	English	prosperous protector
Edmund	Old English	Protector.
Edolf	Old English	A prosperous wolf.
Edom	Hebrew	Red.
Edric	Old English	A prosperous ruler.
Edsel	Teutonic	The noble one.
Edward	Old English	Happy guardian.
Edwardo		Happy guardian.
Edwin	Old English	Prosperous friend.
Efrain	Spanish	Fruitful. One of the sons of Joseph in the Bible.
Efram	Hebrew	Fruitful. One of the sons of Joseph in the Bible.
Efrem	Hebrew	Fruitful. One of the sons of Joseph in the Bible.
Egan	Irish Gaelic	Little fire.
Egbert	Old English	A bright sword.

Egerton	Old English	Edge.
Egeus		From Shakespeare's play Midsummer-Night's Dream.
Egil	Norwegian, French	The edge or point, a sting.
Eglamour		From Shakespeare's play Two Gentlemen of Verona.
Egmont	German	Weapon, defender.
Egon	Teutonic	The tip of a sword.
Egor	Russian	Russian form of George. A tiller of the soil (farmer).
Egyed	Hungarian	Shield bearer.
Ehner	Old English	Noble and famous.
Ehno	Italian from Teutonic	A protector.
Ehnore	Old English	From the riverbank with Elm trees.
Ehren	Teutonic	Honorable.
Ehud	Hebrew	The sympathetic one.
Eideard	Scottish Gaelic	A rich guardian.
Einar	Old Norse	A lone warrior.
Eirik	Norwegian	An all-powerful ruler.
Eisig	Hebrew	He who laughs.
Ekachakra	Hindu	Son of Kashyapa.
Eknath	Hindu	Poet, saint.
Eladio	Latin	A man from Greece.
Elan	Hebrew/ Native American	Hebrew: A tree. North American Indian: The friendly one.
Eland	Old English	From the island.
Elbert	Teutonic	Noble and illustrious.
Elbow		From Shakespeare's play Measure for Measure.
Elden	Old English	An old, wise friend.
Eldin	Old English	An old, wise friend.
Eldon	Old English	From the hill.
Eldred	Old English	A great counselor.
Eldric	Old English	An old, wise ruler.
Eldrich	Old English	An old, wise ruler.
Eldridge	Old English	From the Alder tree ridge.

Eldwin	Old German	Old friend.
Eleazar	Hebrew	God is my help.
Elek	Hungarian	Helper and defender of mankind.
Elezar	Hebrew	God is my help.
Elgan	Welsh	Bright circle.
Elgar	Old English	A noble spear.
Eli	Hebrew	The highest. A Biblical name. Also from the name Elias, Elijah, Elisha.
Elia		The Lord is God.
Elias	Hebrew	The Lord is God. An Israelite prophet in the Bible.
Elijah	Hebrew	The Lord is God.
Eliot		The Lord is God.
Elisha	Hebrew	God is my salvation. The successor of Elijah in the Bible. A boy or girl's name.
Elkan	Hebrew	Possessed by God.
Ellar	Scottish Gaelic	A butler or steward.
Ellard	Teutonic	A noble ruler.
Ellery	Teutonic/Cornish	Teutonic: From the Elder tree. Cornish: A Swan.
Elliot		The Lord is God. From the name Elijah.
Elliott	English from Old French	The Lord is God.
Ellis	English from Greek	A form of Elias. See Elijah.
Ellison	English from Greek	The son of Ellis or Elias. The Lord is God. Also see Elijah.
Elmar	Old English	Famous nobleman.
Elmo	unknown	Protector.
Elner	Teutonic	Famous.
Eloy	Latin	To choose. A Spanish name.
Elroy	English from French	The king. Also see Leroy.
Elsdon	Old English	From the noble one's valley.
Elston	Old English	From the nob one's farm.
Elton	Old English	The old town.

Elu	Native American	Full of grace.
Elvin	Teutonic	All wise.
Elvis	Old Norse	All wise.
Elvy	Old English	An elfin warrior.
Elward	Old English	A noble guardian.
Elwin	Old English	A friend of the elves.
Elwood	Old English	The ruler of the elves.
Ely		The highest.
Emerson		The son of Emery. Ruler of work.
Emery	Teutonic	Ruler of work.
Emil	Teutonic	Industrious. The masculine form of Emily.
Emilio	Italian/Spanish	Industrious. The masculine form of Emily.
Emir	Arabic	Charming prince.
Emlen	Teutonic	Industrious. The masculine form of Emily.
Emlyn	Welsh	Industrious. The masculine form of Emily.
Emmanuel	Hebrew	God is with us. A boy or girl's name.
Emmet	Old English	Industrious. A boy or girl's name.
Emrey	Teutonic	An industrious ruler.
Emrick	Welsh	immortal
Emrys	Welsh	Welsh form of Ambrose. Immortal.
Emyr	Welsh	Honor.
Enda	Irish Gaelic	Bird-like. A boy or girl's name.
Endymion	Greek	A beautiful youth from mythology.
Eneas	Greek	The praised one.
Engelbert	Teutonic	A bright Angel.
Ennis	Celtic	From the island. Also see Innes.
Ennor	Cornish	From the boundary. A boy or girl's name.
Enoch	Hebrew	Experienced, or consecrated. A Biblical name.
Enos	Hebrew	Mankind. A character in the Bible. Also an Irish form of Angus.

Enrico	Italian	In riches or richness.
Enrique	Portuguese/Spanish	The ruler of the home or estate.
Enzo	Italian	From the Laurel tree or crowned with laurels. From the name Lorenzo and other names.
Eoin	Gaelic	Gaelic form of John. God is gracious.
Ephraim	Hebrew	Fruitful. One of the sons of Joseph in the Bible.
Erasmus	Greek	Worthy of love.
Erastus	Greek	The loving one.
Ercole	Italian	From the exceptionally strong mythological hero (Hercules).
Erebus	Greek	The mythological God of darkness.
Erek	Polish	Lovable.
Erhard	Teutonic	Strong and honorable.
Eric	Old Norse	Honorable ruler.
Erik	Norwegian	Honorable ruler.
Erin	Irish Gaelic	From Ireland. A boy or girl's name.
Erith	Old English	From the gravelly landing place. An English location.
Erland	Old Norse	A foreigner, a stranger.
Ermanno	Italian	A man of the army.
Ernest	Teutonic	The serious, earnest one.
Ernie		The serious, earnest one.
Eros	Greek	The God of love.
Errol	Scottish	To wander.
Erroll		To wander.
Erskine	Scottish Gaelic	From the heights.
Eruera	Maori	Maori form of Edward. Happy guardian.
Ervin	Scottish	From a location (Irving).
Erwin	Old English	From the words `boar' and 'friend'.
Eryx	Greek	A mythological figure.
Esau	Hebrew	The hairy one. The son of Isaac and brother of Jacob in the Bible.
Esbern	Old Norse	A divine bear.

Escalus		From Shakespeare's plays Measure for Measure and Romeo & Juliet.
Escanes		From Shakespeare's play Pericles.
Esidor	Greek	The gift of Isis (an Egyptian goddess).
Esmond	Old English	The gracious or handsome protector.
Esra	Hebrew	The helper. A prophet in the Bible.
Essex	Old English	The Saxons from the East. An English county.
Essien	African	Sixth-born son.
Este	Italian	From the East.
Esteban	Spanish	Spanish form of Stephen. A crown or garland.
Estes	Latin	Estuary.
Ethan	Hebrew	Firm, strong.
Ethelred	Teutonic	A noble counselor.
Etienne	French	French form of Stephen.
Eton	Old English	From the estate by the river.
Ettore	Italian	To hold fast. The name of a Trojan hero in classical mythology.
Etzel	Teutonic	The noble one.
Euan	Scottish Gaelic	Possibly meaning born of the Yew tree.
Eudor	Greek	Good gift.
Eugene	Greek	Born lucky.
Eumann	Scottish Gaelic	A prosperous protector. Also see Eamonn.
Euridice	Greek	Justice. In mythology, the love interest of Orpheus.
Eurwyn	Welsh	Fair and golden.
Eusebio	Greek	Pious, respectful.
Eustace	Greek	Fruitful, or steadfast.
Evan	Welsh	Young warrior. Also see John and Owen.
Evander	Greek	A good man. A mythological character.
Evangelos	Greek	The evangelist.

Evelyn	English	From an old surname, but also related to Eve. A boy or girl's name.
Everard	Old English	As strong or brave as a boar. Also see Eberhard.
Everet	Old English	As strong or brave as a boar. Also see Eberhard.
Everett	Old English	As strong or brave as a boar. Also see Eberhard.
Everild	Old English	The slayer of the boar. A boy or girl's name.
Everley	Old English	From the place of the wild boar.
Evzen	Czech	Of noble birth or descent.
Ewald	Teutonic	He who rules by the law.
Ewan	Scottish Gaelic	Possibly meaning born of the Yew tree.
Ewart	Old English	A ewe herder.
Ewing	Old English	A friend of the law.
Eyan		
Eydie		Rich gift.
Ezekiel	Hebrew	God strengthens, or the strength of God. One of the books of the Bible.
Ezio	Latin	Like an eagle.
Ezra	Hebrew	The helper. A prophet in the Bible.
Faber	French	A little blacksmith.
Fabian	Latin	Bean grower.
Fabrice	Latin	A craftsman.
Fabron	French	A little blacksmith.
Fadil	Arabic	The generous or distinguished one.
Fagan	Gaelic	The little fiery one.
Fairfax	Old English	The one with beautiful hair.
Fairley	Old English	A clearing in the woods. A boy or girl's name.
Faisal	Arabic	A wise judge.
Falgun	Hindu	A month in the Hindu calendar.
Falk	Yiddish	The falcon.
Falkner	Old French	A falconer, or falcon handler.

Fallon	Irish	A leader. A boy or girl's name.
Fane	Old English	Eager.
Faraji	African	Consolation.
Farand	Teutonic	Attractive, pleasant.
Farid	Arabic	Unique, unrivaled.
Fariel	Persian	
Farkas	Hungarian	Wolf.
Farley	Old English	From the fern clearing. A boy or girl's name.
Farman	Old Norse	A traveler or hawker.
Farnell	Old English	From the hill of ferns.
Farnley	Old English	From the fern meadow.
Farook	Arabic	One who can tell right from wrong.
Farquhar	Scottish Gaelic	The dear one.
Farrar	Latin	Blacksmith.
Farrell	Celtic	The valorous one.
Farriss	Gaelic	A rock.
Faulkner	Old French	A falconer, or falcon handler.
Faust	Latin	The fortunate one.
Favian	Latin	Understanding.
Faxon	Teutonic	Long hair.
Faysal	Arabic	A wise judge.
Fear	English	
Februus	Latin	A Pagan god.
Fedele	Italian	Faithful.
Federico	Italian/Spanish	A peaceful ruler.
Felipe	Spanish	A lover of horses.
Felix	Latin	Happy and prosperous.
Felton	Old English	From the farm in the field.
Fenn	Old English	A marsh or fen.
Fenton	Old English	From the marshlands.
Fenwick	Old English	From the farm in the marshland.
Feodore	Greek	The gift of God.
Ferdinand	Teutonic	Prepared for the journey. An adventurer or traveler.

Ferenc	Latin, Hungarian	Independent, free
Fergal	Irish Gaelic	A man of valor.
Fergus	Gaelic	Fearghas (Gaelic), Feargus. A Disney cartoon character.
Ferguson	Gaelic	Son of Fergus. Manly.
Fernando		Daring, adventurous.
Fernleigh	Old English	From the fern meadow.
Fernley	Old English	From the fern meadow.
Feroz	Arabic	Victorious and successful.
Ferran	Arabic	Baker.
Ferrand	Old French	A gray-haired man.
Ferrer	Old French	The blacksmith.
Ferris	Gaelic	A rock.
Feste		From Shakespeare's play Twelfth Night.
Festus	Latin	Steadfast.
Ffionn	Welsh	Foxglove Flower
Fiachra	Irish Gaelic	A raven.
Fidel	Latin	Faithful.
Fielding	Old English	A field dweller.
Fife	Scottish	A man from Fife.
Figaro	Latin	Daring, cunning.
Filbert	Teutonic	Very bright.
Filip	Polish	A lover of horses.
Filippo	Italian	A lover of horses.
Finbar	Irish Gaelic	Fair-headed.
Fineas	Egyptian/Hebrew	Egyptian: The Nubian (dark-skinned). Hebrew: An oracle.
Fingal	Scottish Gaelic	The fair stranger.
Finian	Irish Gaelic	Fair or white.
Finlay	Scottish Gaelic	The fair warrior.
Finley		Fair haired one.
Finn	Irish Gaelic/Old Norse	Irish Gaelic: The white or fair one. Old Norse: A man from Finland.
Finnegan	Irish Gaelic	Fair.
Fionn	Celtic	White, fair.

Firdos	Arabic	Paradise.
Firmin	Latin	Steadfast and firm.
Firth	Old English	Of the woodland.
Fisk	Swedish	Fisherman.
Fitch	Old French	A lance or spear.
Fitz	Latin	son
Fitzgerald	Old French	The son of Gerald. A spear warrior.
Fitzhugh	Old French	The son of Hugh. Heart and mind.
Fitzjames	Old French	The son of James. The supplanter.
Fitzpatrick	Old French	The son of Patrick. Nobleman.
Fitzroy	Old French	The son of the king.
Fjodor	Russian	
Flannan	Irish Gaelic	Ruddy, or red-haired.
Flannery		Flat land.
Flavian	Latin	Golden-haired.
Flavius	Latin	Golden-haired.
Fleance		From Shakespeare's play MacBeth.
Fleeting	Old French	A man from Flanders.
Fleming	Old English	A native of Flanders.
Fletcher	Old French	Arrow maker.
Flint	Old English	A hard stone.
Floke	Teutonic, Norse	Guardian of the people.
Florian	Latin	A flower, blooming. The masculine form of flora.
Floritzel		From Shakespeare's play A Winter's Tale.
Floyd	Welsh	The hollow.
Fluellen		From Shakespeare's play Henry V.
Flynn	Irish Gaelic	The red-haired one.
Fodor	Hungarian	Curly haired.
Folant	Welsh	Welsh form of Valentine. Strong, healthy.
Folkus	Hungarian	People, famous.
Fonz	Teutonic	Noble and ready.
Fonzie	Teutonic	Noble and ready.

Forbes	Scottish Gaelic	Prosperous.
Ford	Old English	From the ford or river crossing.
Forest	Old French	Out of the woods.
Forester	Old French	A forester or gamekeeper.
Forrest	Old French	Forest dweller.
Forrester		Of the forest.
Forster		Of the forest.
Fortescue	Old French	A strong shield.
Fortinbras		From Shakespeare's play Hamlet.
Fortunato	Latin	The fortunate one.
Foster	Old English/Old French	Old English: A foster parent. Old French: A shearer.
Francis	Latin	From France, or a free man.
Francis	Latin	From France, or a free man.
Francisco	Spanish	From France, or a free man.
Frank	Teutonic	A member of the tribe of the Franks. Also from the name Francis and Franklin.
Franklin	Old French	Free man.
Frans	Scandinavian	From France, or a free man.
Franz	German	From France, or a free man.
Fraser	Old French	A strawberry, or from a Norman family name.
Frasier		Strawberry.
Frayne	Old French/Old English	Old French: An Ash tree. Old English: Stranger.
Fred	Teutonic	A peaceful ruler. From the name Alfred, Frederick and Wilfred.
Freddie	Teutonic	A peaceful ruler. From the name Alfred, Frederick and Wilfred.
Freddy	Teutonic	A peaceful ruler. From the name Alfred, Frederick and Wilfred.
Frederick	Teutonic	A peaceful ruler.
Free	Old English	In liberty.
Freeman	Old English	A freeborn man.
Fremont	Teutonic	The noble protector.

Frigyes	Hungarian	Peace, might.
Frith	Old English	Of the woodland.
Fritz	German	A peaceful ruler.
Froth		From Shakespeare's play Measure for Measure.
Fudo	Japanese	The God of fire and wisdom.
Fujita	Japanese	Field.
Fulbright		Very light.
Fuller	Old English	A fuller, or cloth-thickener.
Fulton	Old English	From the muddy place.
Furnell	Old French	A furnace.
Fyfe	Scottish	A man from Fife.
Fyodor	Russian	The gift of God.
Gabai	Hebrew	Delight, adornment.
Gable	French	Little Gabriel. A man of God.
Gabor	Hungarian	Hungarian form of Gabriel. A man of God.
Gabriel	Hebrew	God is my strength. One of the archangels in the Bible. A boy or girl's name.
Gadiel	Hebrew	God is my fortune.
Gadil	Arabic	God is my wealth
Gafna	unknown	
Gagan	Hindu	
Gage	Old French	A pledge.
Gair	Irish Gaelic	Short.
Gaius	Latin	To rejoice.
Galahad		From a location in the Bible. One of King Arthur's knights.
Gale		A stranger. A boy or girl's name.
Galen	Greek	The calm one, or the helper. A boy or girl's name.
Galeno	Spanish	Little bright one.
Galip	Turkish	Winner.
Gallagher	Irish Gaelic	The foreign helper.
Gallard	Old French	From gay and lively, or a dandy.

Galloway	Gaelic	A stranger or foreigner.
Gallus		From Shakespeare's play Antony & Cleopatra.
Galor	Old French	From gay and spirited, or a dandy.
Galton	Old English	From the rented estate or farm.
Galvin	Irish Gaelic	The right one.
Galway	Gaelic	A stranger or foreigner.
Gamal	Arabic	Camel.
Gamaliel	Hebrew	The recompense of God. A Biblical name.
Gaman	Hindu	
Gamba	African	Warrior.
Gamble	Norse	Old.
Gamel	Scandinavian	The old one.
Ganan	Aboriginal	From the West.
Gandolf	Teutonic	The progress of the wolf. J.R.R. Tolkien wizard character.
Ganesh	Sanskrit	The lord of the hosts. The elephant-headed Hindu God of wisdom.
Gannon	Irish Gaelic	The little blond or fair one.
Ganymede	Greek	A mythological youth.
Gara	Hungarian	Goshawk.
Gardiner	Old French	One who tends the garden.
Gardner		A gardener.
Gareth	Welsh	Gentle, or an old man.
Garett	Anglo-Saxon	Powerful with the spear.
Garfield	Old English	From the triangular field or battlefield.
Garin	Old German	Warrior.
Garland	Old French	A crown or wreath of flowers. A boy or girl's name.
Garman	Old English	The spearman.
Garmond	Old English	A spear protector.
Garner	Old French	One who tends the garden.
Garnet	Old French	Dark red, from the color of pomegranates. Also the name of a gemstone. A boy or girl's name.

Garrett	English	English from Old French. A spear warrior. Also see Gerald and Gerard.
Garrick	Old English	Leads by the spear.
Garridan	English	You hid.
Garrison		Troops in battle.
Garron		Guardian.
Garry		To watch.
Garth	Old Norse	A field or garden.
Garton	Old Norse	A dweller at the fenced farm.
Garvey	Gaelic	From the rough place.
Garvin	Teutonic	A spear friend.
Garwood	Old English	From the Fir trees.
Gary	English/Teutonic	English: A spearman. Also from the name Gareth, Teutonic: Garfield and Garrett.
Garyson	Old English	Son of Gary
Gaspar	Persian	The master of the treasure. Also see Caspar and Jasper.
Gassy	Old Norse	The staff of the Goths.
Gaston	French	A man from the province of Gascony.
Gaurav	Hindu	
Gautam	Hindu	
Gautama	Sanskrit	The name of the Buddha.
Gautier	French	A mighty ruler.
Gavan		White hawk.
Gavin	Celtic	Little hawk.
Gavrie	Russian	Man of God.
Gavril	Russian	A man of God.
Gawain	Celtic	A battle hawk. One of King Arthur's legendary knights. Also see Gavin.
Gayle	Hebrew	Father's joy. A boy or girl's name.
Gaylord	Old French	Brave.
Geary	Old English	Changeable.
Gedeon	Hungarian	Warrior, devastator.
Geert	Germanic	Brave strength.
Geet	Hindu	

Geir	Norse	Spear.
Gelar	Aboriginal	A brother.
Gene	Greek	Noble, well born. A boy or girl's name.
Genesis	Hebrew	Origin.
Geoff	Teutonic	Divinely peaceful. Derived from Godfrey.
Geoffrey	Teutonic	Divinely peaceful. Derived from Godfrey.
Geordi		Hill near meadows.
Geordie		Hill near meadows.
George	Greek	A tiller of the soil (farmer).
Gerad		Strange understanding of other people.
Geraint	Welsh	Gentle, or an old man.
Gerald	English from Old French	A spear warrior. Also see Garrett and Gerard.
Gerard	English from Old French	A spear warrior, or brave spearman. Also see Garrett and Gerald.
Gerik	Polish	Prosperous spearman.
Germain	Latin	A brother. A male version of Germaine.
Gerome	Greek	A sacred or holy name.
Geronimo	Italian	A sacred or holy name.
Gerry	English from Old French	A spear warrior. A boy or girl's name.
Gershom	Hebrew	In exile. A stranger.
Gervase	Teutonic	A spear servant.
Gerwyn	Welsh	Fair love.
Gerzson	Hungarian	Stranger, banished.
Gethin	Welsh	Dark-skinned.
Ghassan	Arabic	In the prime of youth.
Gi	Korean	The brave one.
Giacobbe	Italian	Italian form of Jacob. Held by the heel.
Giacomo	Italian	The supplanter.
Gianni	Italian	Italian form of John. God is gracious.

Gibson	Old English	Son of Gilbert. Trusted.
Gideon	Hebrew	The mighty warrior. A Biblical name.
Gifford	Teutonic	A gift.
Gilbert	Teutonic	Trusted.
Gilby	Norse	A pledge.
Gilchrist	Gaelic	The servant of Christ.
Giles	Greek	A kid, or young goat.
Gilford	Old English	By the ford.
Gillespie		Servant of the Bishop.
Gillet	French	Little Gilbert. Trusted.
Gilmer	Scottish Gaelic	A servant of the Virgin Mary.
Gilroy	Gaelic	A son of the red-haired man.
Gino	Italian	Short for names ending with Gino.
Ginton	Arabic	A garden.
Giordano	Italian	Flowing down, as in the River Jordan.
Giovanni	Italian	God is gracious.
Giraldo	Italian	A spear warrior. Also see Garrett and Gerard.
Girish	Hindu	
Girra	Aboriginal	A creek, or a tree.
Girvan	Gaelic	The rough little one.
Giulio	Italian	A Roman family name, possibly meaning youthful. Born in July.
Giuseppe	Italian	Italian form of Joseph. God shall add.
Givon	Arabic	Hill, heights.
Gladstone	Old English	A bright rock.
Gladwin	Old English	A bright or kind friend.
Glanville	Old French	From the estate of Oak trees.
Glen	Gaelic/Welsh/Cornish	From the valley or glen. A boy or girl's name.
Glendon	Gaelic	From the fortress it the glen.
Glenn		From the valley or glen.
Glover	Old English	A glove maker.
Glyn	Gaelic/Welsh/Cornish	From the valley or glen.
Glynn	Gaelic/Welsh/Cornish	From the valley or glen.

Goddard	Old English	Divinely brave or strong.
Godfrey	Teutonic	God's peace.
Godwin	Old English	A divine or good friend.
Golding	Old English	The son of the golden one.
Goliath	Hebrew	Revealing.
Gomer	Hebrew/Old English	Hebrew: Complete. Old English: Good and famous.
Gomez	Spanish	A man.
Gonzalo		From Shakespeare's play The Tempest.
Gopal	Sanskrit	The cowherd.
Gordon	Scottish Gaelic	Triangular hill.
Gordy	Scottish Gaelic	Triangular hill. From the name Gordon.
Gore	Old English	From the triangular plot of ground.
Gorman	Teutonic	Blue-eyed.
Goronwy	Welsh	A figure from Celtic mythology.
Gorran	Cornish	A hero.
Gottfried	German	Divinely peaceful. Also see Geoffrey.
Gough	Welsh	Red-haired.
Govinda	Sanskrit	A cowherd, one who is good at finding cows.
Gower	Celtic	Pure.
Grady	Irish Gaelic	Illustrious, noble.
Graeme	Old English	From the gravelly place or homestead. A common Scottish surname.
Graham	Old English	From the gravelly place or homestead. A common Scottish surname.
Granger	Old English	A farmer.
Grant	Old French	The large or tall one.
Grantham	Old English	From the big meadow.
Granville	Old French	Large village.
Gratian	Latin	Pleasing, or thankful.
Gratiano		From Shakespeare's play's Merchant of Venice and Othello.
Grayson	Old English	The son of the bailiff.

Greg		Vigilant, watchful.
Greger	Swedish	Vigilant, watchful.
Gregg		Vigilant, watchful.
Gregory	Greek	Vigilant, watchful.
Gremio		From Shakespeare's play Taming of the Shrew.
Gresham	Old English	From the grazing land.
Greville	Old French	From a location in Normandy.
Griffin		A mythological beast.
Griffith	Welsh	A powerful lord. Also see Gryffyn.
Griswold	Teutonic	From the grey forest.
Grosvenor	Old French	A great huntsman.
Grover	Old English	From the grove, of trees.
Grumio		From Shakespeare's play Taming of the Shrew.
Gryffyn	Comish/Welsh	Mythological beast. A boy or girl's name.
Gugliehno	Italian	A strong and resolute protector.
Guiderius		From Shakespeare's play Cymbeline.
Guido	Italian	The wide one, or from the wood.
Guildenstern		From Shakespeare's play Hamlet.
Guildford	Old English	By the ford.
Guillaume	French	A strong and resolute protector.
Guillermo	Spanish	A strong and resolute protector.
Gul	Hindu	
Gulab	Hindu	
Gunnar	Teutonic	Bold warrior.
Gunther	German	A bold warrior.
Guntur	Indonesian	Thunder.
Gurion	Hebrew	Of lion-like strength, or the place of God.
Gurkan	Turkish	Gurko.
Gus	Old Norse	The staff of the Goths.
Gustav	Old Norse	Lord's cane.
Guthrie	Scottish Gaelic	From the windy place.
Guy	Teutonic	The wide one, or from the wood.

Gwilym	Welsh	Welsh form of William. A strong and resolute protector.
Gwyn	Welsh	White, fair, or blessed. A boy or girl's name.
Gwynfor	Welsh	From the fair place.
Gye	Teutonic	The wide one, or from the wood.
Gyles	Greek	A kid, or young goat.
Gyula	Hungarian	Of a honor.
Ha-Neul	Korean	Sky.
Habib	Arabic	The beloved one.
Hackett	German	Little woodsman.
Hadar	unknown	Glorious.
Hadden	English	Child of the heather-filled valley.
Haddon	Old English	From the heathery hill.
Hadi	Arabic	A guide or leader.
Hadley	Old English	From the heathery field.
Hadrian	Latin	The dark one or a man from the sea, as in the Adriatic. The name of six Popes.
Hadwin	Old English	A friend in battle.
Hafiz	Arabic	The guardian.
Hagan	Teutonic	Strong defense.
Hagen	Irish Gaelic	Little Hugh. Heart and mind.
Hagley	Old English	From the hay wood clearing.
Hahn	German	Rooster.
Haig	Old English/Teutonic	From the enclosure or paddock.
Haile	hero	
Haines	Old English	From the fenced area.
Hakan	Norse, Turkish	Noble, fiery.
Hakim	Arabic	Wise and judicious.
Hakon	Old Norse	Of noble birth.
Hal		Estate ruler.
Halbert	Old English	A brilliant hero.
Halden	Old English	Half Danish.
Haldor	Old Norse	Rock of Thor (the Norse God of thunder).

Hale	Old English	The dweller in the nook.
Haley	Irish Gaelic	Ingenious. A boy or girl's name.
Halford	Old English	From the ford in the nook.
Halian	Zuni Indian	Of Julius.
Halifax	Old English	From the Holy field. A city in Northern England and a seaport in Canada.
Halil	Turkish	
Hall	Old English	From the manor house or hall.
Hallam	Old Norse	The dweller at the rocks.
Halse	Old English	From the neck of land.
Halsey	Old English	From Hal's island.
Halstead	Old English	The stronghold.
Halsten	Old Norse	A rock.
Halton	Old English	
Halvard	Old Norse	The defender of the rock.
Hamal	Arabic	As gentle as a lamb.
Hamar	Old Norse	Ingenious.
Hamid	Arabic	The thankful one.
Hamilton	Old English	From the crooked hill.
Hamish	Scottish	Scottish form of James. The supplanter.
Hamlet	Old English	From the enclosed land. Also the name of a famous Shakespearean character and play.
Hamlin	Teutonic	From the small home.
Hamon	Greek	The faithful one.
Hampton	Old English	From the river meadow.
Hanan	Hebrew	Arabic: The affectionate one. Hebrew: The gracious gift of God. A boy or girl's name.
Handel	German	Little Hans. God is gracious. Also the name of a famous composer.
Hanford	Old English	From the rocky ford.
Hani	Arabic	The contented one.

Hank		The ruler of the home or estate. Also see Harrison, Henderson and Parry.
Hanke		The ruler of the home or estate. From the name Henry.
Hanley	Old English	From the high clearing.
Hannes	Hebrew	God is gracious.
Hannibal	Phoenician	The famous general of Carthage (Northern Africa) who crossed the Alps and invaded Italy.
Hannu	Finnish	Finnish form of John.
Hans	German	God is gracious.
Hansel	German	God is gracious. From the name Hans.
Hansi	German	God is gracious.
Hanson	Old English/Teutonic	Son of Hans. God is gracious.
Haral	Old Norse	Army power, or ruler of the army.
Harald	Scandinavian	Army power, or ruler of the army.
Harcourt	Old English	The dweller at the falconer's cottage.
Harden	Old English	From the valley of the hare.
Hardik	Hindu	
Harding	Old English	A brave warrior.
Hardwin	Old English	A brave friend.
Hardy	Teutonic	Bold, daring.
Hare	Maori	Maori form of Charles. Manly, full grown.
Haresh	Hindu	
Harford	Old English	The ford of the stag.
Hargreave	Old English	From the hare grove.
Hari	Sanskrit	He who removes evil. Exorcist.
Harish	Hindu	
Harith	North African	Cultivator.
Harlan	Old English	From the rocky land.
Harleigh	Old English	From the hare or stag meadow.
Harley	Old English	From the hare or stag meadow. A boy or girl's name.
Harlow	Old English	From the fortified hill.
Harman	Teutonic	A man of the army.

Harold	Old Norse	Army power, or ruler of the army.
Haroun	Arabic	Arabic forms of Aaron.
Harper	Old English	A harp player or maker. A boy or girl's name.
Harrison	Old English	Son of Harry. Army power, or ruler of the army.
Harry		Army power, or ruler of the army.
Harsh	Hindu	Joy.
Hart	unknown	Deer, stag.
Hartley	English	From the deer pasture.
Hartman	Teutonic	The strong man.
Hartwell	Old English	From the well.
Hartwin	German	A brave fiend.
Hartwood	Old English	From the forest of stags.
Haru	Japanese	Born in the spring.
Harun	Arabic	Arabic forms of Aaron.
Harvey	Breton	Army warrior.
Harwin	Old English	A brave friend.
Harwood	Old English	From the wood of the hares.
Hasad	Turkish	Harvest.
Hasim	Arabic	The decisive one.
Haslett	Old English	From the Hazel tree wood.
Hassan	Arabic	Handsome and good.
Hastin	Hindu	elephant
Hastings	German	Swift one.
Havelock	Old Norse	Sea sport.
Haven	Old English	A place of refuge.
Havika	Hawaiian	Beloved.
Hawley	Old English	From the hedged meadow.
Hayden	Old English	From the heathery hill.
Hayes	Old English	From the hedged area.
Hayward	Teutonic	The brave one, or the chief guardian.
Haywood	Old English	From the fenced wood.
Hazlett	Old English	From the Hazel tree wood.
Hazlitt	Old English	From the Hazel tree wood.

Hearst	Old English	A dweller in the wood.
Heath	Old English	The heath-land dweller.
Heathcliff	English	From the cliff-land heath. The hero of Emily Browns Wuthering Heights.
Heathcote	Old English	From the cottage on a heath.
Hecate		From Shakespeare's play MacBeth.
Hector	Greek	To hold fast. The name of a Trojan hero in classical mythology.
Heddwyn	Welsh	Blessed peace.
Hedley	Old English	A clearing in the heather.
Heilyn	Welsh	A steward.
Heinrich	German	German form of Henry. The ruler of the home or estate.
Heinz		Ruler of the home. From the name Heinrik.
Helaku	Native American	Sunny day.
Helenus		From Shakespeare's play Troilus & Cressida.
Helicanus		From Shakespeare's play Pericles.
Helio	Latin	The sun.
Heller	Old German	The sun.
Helmut	Teutonic	A courageous protector.
Helmuth	German	Helmet, protector, courage.
Hemal	Hindu	
Hemang	Hindu	
Hemant	Hindu	
Hemendra	Hindu	
Hemi	Maori	Maori form of James. The supplanter.
Henderson	Old English from Teutonic	The son of Henry. The ruler of the home or estate.
Hendra	Cornish	From the old farm.
Hendy	Old English	The courteous one.
Henleigh	Old English	From the high clearing.
Henley	Old English	From the high clearing.
Henning	Teutonic	Ruler of an estate.
Henri	French	The ruler of the home or estate.

Henrik		Ruler of the home.
Henry	Teutonic	The ruler of the home or estate.
Herb		Bright, excellent army or ruler.
Herbert	Teutonic	Bright, excellent army or ruler.
Hercules	Greek	The exceptionally strong mythological hero.
Herman	Teutonic	Person of high rank.
Hermes	Greek	The messenger of the gods.
Hermon	Teutonic	A man of the army.
Hernando	Spanish	Prepared for the journey. An adventurer or traveller.
Herold	Old Norse	Army power, or ruler of the army.
Herrick	Old Norse	The army ruler.
Hershel	Jewish	A deer.
Herst	Old English	A dweller in the wood.
Hertford	Old English	The ford of the stag.
Herve	French	Battle-worthy.
Hervey	Breton	Battle-worthy.
Herwin	Teutonic	A battle companion.
Hesketh	Old Norse	From the horseracing track.
Hew	Teutonic	Heart and mind. Also see Hagen, Hubert and Hudson.
Hewett	Teutonic	Little Hugh. Heart and mind.
Hewie	Scottish	Heart and mind. Also see Hagen, Hubert and Hudson.
Hewston	Old English	From the place of Hugh.
Heyward	Teutonic	The brave one, or the chief guardian.
Hiatt	Old English	A high gate.
Hieronymus	German	German form of Jerome. A sacred or holy name.
Hilary	Latin	The cheerful one. A boy or girl's name.
Hildebrand	Teutonic	A battle sword.
Hillel	Hebrew	The praised one. A Biblical name.
Hilton	Old English	From the farm on the hill.
Hippolyte	Greek	He who frees the horses.

Hiram	Hebrew	Exalted. A name from the Bible.
Hiroshi	Japanese	Generous.
Hirsh	Jewish	A deer.
Hiten	Hindu	
Hitendra	Hindu	
Hitesh	Hindu	
Ho	Chinese/Korean	Goodness.
Hobart	Teutonic	A brilliant mind.
Hogan	Irish Gaelic	A youth.
Holbrook	Old English	From the brook in the valley.
Holden	Old English	From the deep valley.
Holger	Old Norse	Spear-like.
Holgernes		From Shakespeare's play Love's Labour's Lost.
Hollis	Old English	From the grove of Holly trees.
Holman	Old English	A dweller in the hollow.
Holmes	Old English	From the island in the river.
Holofernes		From Shakespeare's play Love's Labour's Lost.
Holt	Old English	A dweller in the wood.
Homer		The name of the epic Greek poet, possibly meaning a pledge.
Hont	Hungarian	Dog breeder, friend of dogs
Hopkin	Welsh	The son of Robert. Famous, bright fame.
Horace	Latin	Hour in time.
Horatio	Latin	Hour in time.
Hori	Polynesian	Polynesian form of George. A tiller of the soil (farmer).
Horst	German	From the wood or wooded hill.
Hortensio	Latin	The garden lover.
Hortensius	Latin	The garden lover.
Horton	Old English	From the grey or muddy place.
Hosea	Hebrew	Salvation.
Houghton	Old English	From the farm on the hill.

Houston	Old English	From the place of Hugh. Also the name of a city in Texas.
Howard	Teutonic	Guardian of the home.
Howe	Old Norse	A hillock or burial mound.
Howell	Cornish/Welsh	The eminent one. Also see Powel.
Howie		Guardian of the home.
Hridayesh	Hindu	
Hrishikesh	Hindu	
Hsin	Chinese	After an ancient dynasty.
Huatare	Maori	The name of a famous chief.
Huba	Hungarian	
Hubert	Teutonic	A brilliant mind.
Hudson	Old English	The son of Hugh. Heart and mind.
Huey		Heart and mind. Also see Hagen, Hubert and Hudson.
Hugh	Teutonic	Heart and mind. Also see Hagen, Hubert and Hudson.
Hugo	Dutch/German	Heart and mind. Also see Hagen, Hubert and Hudson.
Humbert	Teutonic	A famous warrior.
Hume	Old English	From the river island.
Humphrey	Teutonic	The protector of the peace.
Hunor	Hungarian	Name of an ethnic group.
Hunter	Old English	The huntsman.
Huntley	Old English	From the hunter's meadow.
Huon		The name of a Tasmanian river and a type of tree. A boy or girl's name.
Hurst	Old English	A dweller in the wood.
Hussain	Arabic	The handsome little one.
Hussein	Arabic	The handsome little one.
Hutton	Old English	From the farm on the hill.
Huw	Welsh	Heart and mind. Also see Hagen, Hubert and Hudson.
Huxley	Old English	The inhospitable place.
Hyam	Hebrew	Life.
Hyatt	Old English	A high gate.

Hyde	English	A hide (an old measurement) of land.
Hylton	Old English	From the farm on the hill.
Hymen		From Shakespeare's play As You Like It.
Hyram	Hebrew	Exalted. A name from the Bible.
Hywel	Cornish/Welsh	The eminent one. Also see Powel.
Iachima		From Shakespeare's play Merry Wives of Windsor.
Iagan	Scottish	The little fiery one.
Iago	Spanish	Spanish form of James. The supplanter. Also from Shakespeare's play Othello.
Iain	Gaelic	God's gracious gift
Ian	Hebrew	God is gracious. The Scottish form of John.
Ibeamaka	African	The agnates are splendid.
Ibrahim	Hebrew	The father of many.
Icarus	Greek	A legendary figure.
Ichabod	Hebrew	The glory has departed.
Iden	Old English	Prosperous.
Idris	Arabic/Welsh	Arabic: A good man. Welsh: A fiery, impulsive lord.
Idwal	Welsh	The lord of the wall or rampart.
Iestin	Welsh	Welsh form of Justin. Just or true.
Iestyn	Welsh	Welsh form of Justin. Just or true.
Ieuan	Welsh	Welsh form of John. God is gracious. Also see Evan and Owen.
Ifor	Welsh	A traditional name of uncertain meaning.
Ignacio	Latin	One who is lively.
Ignatius	Latin	Ardent, fiery.
Igor	Scandinavian	Hero. Also a Russian variation of the name George.
Ihorangi	Polynesian	Rain.
Ike	Hebrew	Laughter, the laughing one.
Ikey	Hebrew	Laughter, the laughing one.

Ilar	Welsh	Cheerful.
Ilario	Italian	Cheerful.
Ilhan	Turkish	
Ilias	Latin	Jehovah is my God
Ilie	Romanian	Romanian form of Elias. The Lord is God.
Ilya	Russian	Russian form of Elijah. The Lord is God.
Imam	Arabic	One who believes in God. A boy or girl's name.
Immanuel	German	God is with us.
Imre	Hungarian	An industrious ruler.
Ince	Latin	Innocent.
Indra	Sanskrit	The God of the atmosphere and sky.
Ingemar	Old Norse	A famous son.
Inger	Old Norse	A son's army or a Hero's daughter. A boy or girl's name.
Inglebert	Teutonic	A bright Angel.
Ingmar	Scandinavian	Famous son.
Ingo		
Ingolf		
Ingram	Teutonic	The raven.
Inigo	Latin	Ardent, fiery.
Innes	Celtic/Gaelic	An island in the river, or from the island. Also see Ennis.
Innocent	Latin	Harmless, innocent. The name of several saints and popes.
Ioannes	Greek	Greek form of John.
Iolo	Welsh	A handsome lord.
Iolyn	Welsh	A handsome lord.
Ion	Romanian	Romanian form of John. God is gracious.
Iorweth	Welsh	A handsome lord.
Ira	Hebrew	Watchful, vigilant. A Biblical name.
Iravan	Hindu	Son of Arjuna and Uloopi.
Irawaru	Polynesian	A figure from legend.

Irvin	Anglo-Saxon	Lover of the sea.
Irving	Scottish	Handsome and fair.
Irwin	Old English	From the words `boar' and 'friend'.
Isa	Sanskrit/Teutonic	Sanskrit: A lord. Teutonic: Strong-willed. A boy or girl's name.
Isaac	Hebrew	Laughter, the laughing one. The son of Abraham in the Bible.
Isaiah	Hebrew	God is salvation, or God is my helper. One of the prophets in the Bible. Lived in the 8th century BC.
Isha	Hindu	One who protects.
Ishmael	Hebrew	The Lord will hear. The first son of Abraham in the Bible.
Ishver	Hindu	
Isidore	Greek	The gift of Isis (an Egyptian goddess).
Isidro	Spanish	Chidro (a river).
Israel	Hebrew	The Lord's soldier.
Istvan	Hungarian	Hungarian form of Stephen. A crown or garland.
Itzaak	Hebrew	Laughter, the laughing one.
Itzak	Hebrew	Laughter.
Itziamar		
Itzik	Hebrew	Laughter, the laughing one.
Ivan		Eastern European form of John.
Ivar	Old Norse	A battle archer.
Ives	Old English	The little archer.
Ivo	German	The little archer.
Ivor	Old Norse	A battle archer.
Izaak	Dutch	Laughter, the laughing one.
Jabari	Swahili	The brave one.
Jabez	Hebrew	Sorrowful.
Jabir	Arabic	The comforter.
Jace	Greek	The healer.
Jacek	Polish	A lily. A male form of hyacinth.
Jack	Hebrew	From the name John, but also used as an independent name. God is gracious.

Jackson	Old English	Son of Jack. God is gracious.
Jacob	Hebrew	Held by the heel.
Jacques	French	French form of Jacob and James.
Jacy	Native American	The moon.
Jaedon		
Jael	Hebrew	To ascend or a wild goat. A boy or girl's name.
Jafar	Hindu	Little stream.
Jagdish	Sanskrit	The ruler of the world.
Jagger	Middle English	A carter or hawker.
Jago	Cornish	Cornish form of James.
Jaiden	English	A modern name derived from Jai or Jay.
Jaidev	Hindu	
Jaidon	English	A modern name derived from Jai or Jay.
Jaime	French	French for I love you. A boy or girl's name.
Jake		Held by the heel. From the name Jacob, but also used as an independent name.
Jakob	Dutch/German/Scandinavian	The supplanter. One who takes the place of another. A Biblical name. Also see James.
Jakub	Czech/Polish	The supplanter. One who takes the place of another. A Biblical name. Also see James.
Jal	English	Wanderer.
Jaleel	Arabic	Great, fine.
Jalen	Arabic	
Jalil	Arabic	Majestic.
Jamal	Arabic	The handsome one. A boy or girl's name.
James	Hebrew	The supplanter. A form of Jacob.
Jamie		The supplanter.
Jamieson	Old English	The son of James. The supplanter.
Jamison	English	son of James

Jan		God is gracious. A boy or girl's name.
Janak	Hindu	
Janardan	Hindu	
Janus	Latin	The Roman God of doors and gates (beginnings and endings). The month of January is derived from this name.
Japhet	Hebrew	Youthful. A son of Noah in the Bible.
Jaques	French	French form of Jacob and James.
Jared	Hebrew	The descendant.
Jarek	Polish	Born in January.
Jarel	French	A location.
Jarlath	Irish Gaelic	A leader or prince.
Jarman	Celtic	A man from Germany.
Jaron	Hebrew	To sing.
Jaroslav	Slavonic	The glory of spring. A popular Czech name.
Jarrad	Hebrew	The descendant.
Jarrah	Aboriginal	A type of Eucalyptus tree. A boy or girl's name.
Jarratt	Teutonic	A spearman.
Jarred	Hebrew	The descendant.
Jarrod	Hebrew	The descendant.
Jarvis	Teutonic	A spear servant.
Jaryn	Gaelic	Jar.
Jason	Greek	The healer. The mythological hero who retrieved the golden fleece.
Jasper	Persian	The treasurer. The name of a gemstone. Also see Caspar and Gaspar.
Jatin	Hindu	
Java		An Indonesian island.
Javan	Latin	angel of Greece
Javed	Persian	Eternal. A popular Muslim name.
Javier	Portuguese/Spanish	Of the new house.

Jay	Sanskrit/Old English	Sanskrit: Victory. Old English: A bird. Also used as a nickname for Jacob, James and many names.
Jayant	Hindu	Victorious, a Rudra.
Jayden	English	God has heard.
Jaysukh	Hindu	
Jayvyn	African	Light spirit.
Jean	French	God is gracious. A boy or girl's name.
Jed	Hebrew	Beloved of God. From the name Jedediah, but also used independently.
Jedd	Hebrew	Beloved of God. From the name Jedediah, but also used independently.
Jedediah	Hebrew	Beloved of God. A Biblical name.
Jedidiah	Hebrew	Beloved of the Lord.
Jedrek	Polish	Strong, manly.
Jeevan	Hindu	Life.
Jeff	Teutonic	Divinely peaceful. Derived from Godfrey.
Jefferson	Old English	The son of Jeffrey. Divinely peaceful. See Geoffrey.
Jeffrey	Teutonic	Divinely peaceful. Derived from Godfrey.
Jehosophat	Hebrew	The Lord judges.
Jelani	African	Mighty.
Jenkins		
Jens	Danish/Norwegian	God is gracious.
Jensen	Nordic	God is gracious
Jerald	English from Old French	A spear warrior. Also see Garrett and Gerard.
Jerara	Aboriginal	Falling water.
Jered	Hebrew	The descendant.
Jeremiah	Hebrew	Appointed by God.
Jeremias	Dutch/German/Spanish	Appointed by God from the Biblical name Jeremiah.
Jeremy	Hebrew	God will uplift.
Jeri	Jeris	

Jericho		Moon city.
Jermain		From Germany. A boy or girl's name.
Jermyn	Cornish	A saint's name.
Jerod		Descendant.
Jerold	English from Old French	A spear warrior. Also see Garrett and Gerard.
Jerolin	Latin	holy name
Jerome	Greek	A sacred or holy name.
Jerrard	English from Old French	A spear warrior, or brave spearman. Also see Garrett and Gerald.
Jerrie	English from Old French	A spear warrior. From the name Gerald, Gerard, Jeremy and Jerome. Also used independently.
Jerry	English from Old French	A spear warrior. From the name Gerald, Gerard, Jeremy and Jerome. Also used independently.
Jervaise	Teutonic	A spear servant.
Jervis	Teutonic	A spear servant.
Jerzy	Polish	Polish form of George. A tiller of the soil (farmer).
Jesse	Hebrew	God's gift. A boy or girl's name.
Jesus	Hebrew	The savior or God is salvation. A variation of Joshua, and a popular Spanish and Portuguese name.
Jet	Latin	Black, the name of a material used for making jewelery. A boy or girl's name.
Jethro	Hebrew	Outstanding, excellent.
Jetmir	Albanian	
Jibril	Arabic	Archangel Gabriel.
Jiger	Hindu	
Jilesh	Hindu	
Jim		The supplanter. A form of Jacob. From the name James.
Jimmie		The supplanter. A form of Jacob. From the name James.
Jimmy		The supplanter. A form of Jacob. From the name James.

Jimuta	Hindu	one of 108 names of the Sun God
Jin	Chinese/Korean	Chinese: Golden. Korean: A jewel. A boy or girl's name.
Jinesh	Hindu	
Jiri	Czech	Czech form of George.
Jiro	Japanese	Second male.
Jirra	Aboriginal	A kangaroo. A boy or girl's name.
Jiten	Hindu	
Jitender	Sanskrit	The powerful conqueror.
Jitendra	Hindu	
Jivana	Hindu	one of 108 names of the Sun God
Jivin	Hindu	to give life
Jo	Hebrew	God shall add. Nickname of Joseph.
Joab	Hebrew	Praise the Lord.
Joachim	Hebrew	Established by God. The name of a king of Judah in the Bible.
Joakim	Hebrew	The Lord will judge.
Job	Hebrew	The persecuted one. A name that is associated with patience.
Jocelin	Latin	The merry one. More commonly a girl's name.
Jock	Scottish	Short form of Jacob or John. God is gracious.
Jody	Hebrew	God shall add. Nickname of Joseph.
Joe	Hebrew	God shall add. Nickname of Joseph.
Joel	Hebrew	God is willing.
Joey	Hebrew	God shall add. Nickname of Joseph.
Joh	Hebrew	God is gracious.
Johann	German	God is gracious.
Johannes	German	God is gracious.
John	Hebrew	God is gracious. The name of many saints. Also see Ian, Jack, Jonathan and Owen.
Johnny		God is gracious. The name of many saints. Also see Ian, Jack, Jonathan and Owen.

Johnson	English	Son of John. God is gracious.
Jolyon	English	English form of Julius. Also suitable for a child born in July.
Jon	Swedish	God is gracious. The name of many saints. Also see Ian, Jack, Jonathan and Owen.
Jonah	Hebrew	A dove. A man of peace.
Jonathan	Hebrew	God has given, or a gift of the Lord. The friend o David in the Bible. Also see John.
Jonny		God is gracious. The name of many saints. Also see Ian, Jack, Jonathan and Owen.
Joo-Chan	Korean	praise the Lord
Joost	Dutch	Fair and just.
Joram	Hebrew	The Lord is exalted.
Jordan	Hebrew	Flowing down, as in the River Jordan. A boy or girl's name.
Jorge	Portuguese/Spanish	A farmer. St George is the patron saint of England.
Jorgen	Danish/Swedish	A farmer. St George is the patron saint of England.
Jorma	Finnish	Appointed by God from the Biblical name Jeremiah.
Jory	Cornish	Cornish form of George. Also from the name Joram.
Jose	Spanish	Spanish form of Joseph. God shall add.
Josef	Czech/Dutch/German/Scandinavian	God will increase.
Joseph	Hebrew	God shall add. The father of Jesus and husband of Mary in the Bible.
Joshua	Hebrew	God is salvation. The Biblical figure who led the Israelites to the promised land. Also see Hosea and Jesus.
Josiah	Hebrew	God heals. A Biblical name.

Joss	Latin	The merry one. From the name Jocelin. Also used as an independent name.
Jourdain	French	Flowing down, as in the River Jordan.
Jourdan	Hebrew	Flowing down, as in the River Jordan.
Jove		
Jowan	Cornish	God is gracious.
Jozef	Polish	God shall add.
Jozsef	Hungarian	God shall add.
Juan	Spanish	Spanish form of John. God is gracious.
Judah	Hebrew	The praised one. A son of Jacob in the Bible.
Judd	Hebrew	Praised.
Jude	Hebrew	Praise.
Julian	English	Youthful.
Julius	Latin	A Roman family name, possibly meaning youthful. Born in July.
Juma	African	Born on a Friday.
Jung	Korean	Righteous.
Junior		The young, child.
Junius	Latin	Born in June.
Jurgen	German	German form of George. A tiller of the soil (farmer).
Justin	Latin	Just or true.
Justus	Latin	Justice.
Jyotis	Sanskrit	Light.
Kabir	Hindu	
Kabos	Hebrew	Swindler.
Kada	Hungarian	
Kadin	Arabic	Friend, companion.
Kadir	Arabic	Powerful.
Kadosa	Hungarian	
Kahn	Hindu	
Kahoku	Hawaiian	Star.
Kai	Hawaiian, Navajo Indian	Sea, willow tree.

Kaikara	Ugandan	Traditional name of God.
Kailash	Hindu	
Kain	Irish Gaelic	Warlike.
Kalani	Hawaiian	Of the Heavens.
Kalb	Arabic	Dog.
Kalden	Tibetan/Sherpa	Of the golden age.
Kale	Hawaiian	Strong and manly, masculine.
Kaleb	Hebrew	The devoted one.
Kaleo	pure	
Kalid	Arabic	Eternal.
Kalidas	Hindu	The poet, musician.
Kalil	Arabic	Good, best friend.
Kalkin	Hindu	10th incarnation of God Vishnu.
Kalman	Hungarian	Strong and manly, masculine.
Kalpanath	Hindu	
Kalti	Aboriginal	A spear.
Kama	Sanskrit/Thai	Sanskrit: The golden one. Thai: Love. A boy or girl's name.
Kamadev	Hindu	God of love
Kamal	Arabic	Perfect.
Kami	Aboriginal	A prickly lizard.
Kamil	Arabic/Czech	Arabic: Perfect. Czech: From a Roman family name. A boy or girl's name.
Kamlesh	Hindu	
Kanak	Hindu	Gold.
Kanan	Hindu	
Kanaye	Japanese	Zealous one.
Kane	Irish Gaelic	Warlike. A boy or girl's name.
Kaniel	Arabic/Hebrew	Arabic: Spear-like. Hebrew: A reed.
Kano	Japanese	The God of the waters.
Kapil	Hindu	Name of a rishi.
Kaplony	Hungarian	Tiger.
Kapolcs	Hungarian	
Karan	Sanskrit	A warrior.

Kardal	Arabic	Mustard seed.
Kardos	Hungarian	Swordsman.
Karel	Czech/Dutch	A free person. A boy or girl's name.
Kari	Aboriginal	Smoke.
Karim	Arabic	Noble and generous.
Karl	German/Scandinavian	A free man.
Karma	Tibetan/Sherpa	A star. A boy or girl's name.
Karol	Polish	A free person. A boy or girl's name.
Karsa	Hungarian	Falcon.
Karsten	German	A follower of Christ. A Christian.
Kartal	Hungarian	Eagle.
Kartik	Hindu	
Kartikeya	Hindu	Son of Shiva and Parvati
Kasch	German	Like a blackbird.
Kasen	Latin	Protected by a helmet.
Kasey	Irish Gaelic	The vigilant one.
Kasim	Arabic	One who shares or distributes.
Kasimir	German	The great destroyer.
Kaspar	German	The treasurer. The name of one of the three wise men in the new testament. Also see Gaspar and Jasper.
Kasper	Polish	The treasurer. The name of one of the three wise men in the new testament. Also see Gaspar and Jasper.
Kateb	Arabic	Writer, author.
Kathel	Irish Gaelic	A battle ruler.
Kauri	Polynesian	A New Zealand tree.
Kaushal	Hindu	
Kaushik	Hindu	
Kavan	Irish Gaelic	The handsome one.
Kavi	Hindu	Poet.
Kay	Welsh	Rejoiced in. A boy or girl's name.
Kayin	Yoruban	Celebrated child.
Kayne	Irish Gaelic	Warlike.
Kazimir	Czech	The great destroyer.
Kean	Irish Gaelic	Ancient. Also see Keane.

Keane	Old English	Handsome and bold.
Kearney	Celtic	Warrior.
Keary	Celtic	Father's dark child.
Keaton		
Kedar	Arabic	Powerful.
Keefe	Irish Gaelic	Handsome, noble.
Keegan	Irish Gaelic	Fiery, determined.
Keeland	Gaelic	Little and slender.
Keeley	Irish Gaelic	Beautiful. A boy or girl's name.
Keenan	Irish Gaelic	Little, ancient.
Keeran	Irish Gaelic	Dark, black.
Kees	Dutch	Horn-colored. From the name Cornelius.
Kegan	Celtic	Fiery.
Keir	Scottish/Celtic	Scottish: Probably from the surname Kerr. Celtic: Dark.
Keiran	Irish Gaelic	Little and dark.
Keith	Celtic	The wind.
Kelan	Irish Gaelic	Slender.
Kelby	Old German	From the farm by the spring or ridge.
Keled	Hungarian	
Keleman	Hungarian	Gentle, kind, docile.
Kell	Old Norse	From the well or spring.
Kellen	German	Swamp.
Keller	Irish Gaelic	Little companion.
Kelly	Irish Gaelic	A warrior. A boy or girl's name.
Kelsey	Old Norse	A dweller on the island or by the water. A boy or girl's name.
Kelso	Scottish	A Scottish town.
Kelt	Greek	A Celtic person.
Kelvin	Scottish/English	Friend of ships.
Kemal	Arabic	Perfect.
Kembell	Celtic	Warrior chief.
Kemble	Celtic	Warrior chief.
Kemenes	Hungarian	Furnace maker.

Kemp	Old English	A warrior, or champion.
Ken	Scottish Gaelic	Handsome and fair, or born of fire. From the name Kenneth and other names beginning with `Ken'.
Kenan	Cornish	The name of a legendary Cornish king.
Kendall	English	Valley of the river Kent.
Kende	Hungarian	Name of an honor.
Kendra	Celtic	Loving male.
Kendrick	Celtic/Old English	Celtic: A hill. Old English: Royal power.
Kenelm	Old English	A brave friend or protector.
Kenley	Old English	From the royal meadow.
Kenn	Welsh/Celtic	Clear as bright water.
Kennard	Old English	Bold and hardy.
Kennedy	Irish Gaelic	Royal.
Kenneth	Scottish Gaelic	Handsome and fair, or born of fire.
Kenny	Scottish Gaelic	Handsome and fair, or born of fire.
Kenrich	Welsh, Old English	Chief hero; royal ruler.
Kenrick	Old English	A bold ruler.
Kent	Celtic	Bright, white. Also from the English county, and from the name Kenneth.
Kenton	Old English	From the royal manor or estate.
Kenver	Cornish	A great chief.
Kenward	Old English	A bold guardian, a brave soldier.
Kenwyn	Cornish/Welsh	The name of a saint. A boy or girl's name.
Kenya	African	The name of an African country. A boy or girl's name.
Kenyon	Irish Gaelic	White or fair-haired.
Keon	African	
Keona	Hawaiian	God's gracious gift.
Keoni	Polynesian	The righteous one.
Ker	English	House.
Kerby	Teutonic/Old Norse	From the church village.
Kerecsen	Hungarian	Falcon.
Kereteki	Polynesian	A mythological figure.

Kermit	Gaelic/Irish Gaelic	A free man.
Kern	Irish Gaelic	The little dark one.
Kernick	Cornish	From the little corner.
Kernow	Cornish	From Cornwall.
Kerr	Norse	Marshland.
Kerrin	Irish Gaelic	Dark, black.
Kerry	Irish Gaelic	The dark one. Also the name of an Irish county. A boy or girl's name.
Kers	Todas Indian	Name of a plant.
Kersen	Indonesian	A cherry.
Kerwin	Irish Gaelic	The little black-haired one.
Keshav	Hindu	Krishna's name
Kester	Scottish	Scottish form of Christopher. Bearing Christ.
Ketan	Hindu	Pebble.
Keve	Hungarian	The name of a saint and a location. A boy or girl's name.
Keverne	Irish Gaelic	Handsome, beautiful.
Kevin	Irish Gaelic	Guiding, leading.
Keyon	Old English	Kingly, regal.
Khairi	Swahili	Eternal.
Khalid	Arabic	Successor.
Khalif	Arabic	A friend.
Khalil	Arabic	Sun.
Khorshed	Persian	Perfection.
Khortdad	Persian	Priest
Khoury	Arabic	Barrel maker.
Kiefer	German	Dark, black.
Kieran	Irish	Permanent, always there. Also the name of a Sydney suburb.
Killara	Aboriginal	The little warlike one.
Killian	Irish Gaelic	The golden one or from the meadow.. A boy or girl's name.
Kim	Vietnamese	Warrior chief.
Kimball	Celtic	

Kimberley	Old English	From the meadow. A boy or girl's name.
Kin	Japanese	Golden.
King	English	A ruler, a sovereign.
Kinga		
Kingsley	Old English	From the king's wood or meadow.
Kingston	Old English	From the king's town.
Kinnard	Irish Gaelic	From the high hill.
Kinnel	Gaelic	Dweller at the head of the cliff.
Kinsey	Old English	A victorious king or prince.
Kintan	Hindu	Wearing a crown.
Kipling	Middle English	One who cures salmon or herring.
Kipp	English	The dweller on the pointed hill.
Kiran	Sanskrit	A ray of light.
Kirby	Teutonic/Old Norse	From the church village. A boy or girl's name.
Kirill	Russian	Lordly.
Kirit	Hindu	Crown, tiara.
Kirk	Old Norse	A dweller by the church.
Kirkley	Old English	From the church meadow.
Kirkwood	Old English	From the church wood.
Kiron	Greek	A wise teacher.
Kirwin	Irish Gaelic	The little black-haired one.
Kisho	Japanese	one who knows his own mind
Kishore	Hindu	
Kit	Greek	Bearing Christ or pure. A boy or girl's name.
Kito	Swahili	A jewel.
Kitto	Cornish	Bearing Christ. From the name Christopher.
Kiva	Hebrew	Protected.
Kiyoshi	Japanese	The quiet one.
Klaas	Dutch	The victory of the people.
Klaes	Frisian	The victory of the people.
Klaud	Latin	The lame one.
Klaus	Greek	Leader in victory.

Klea		
Klemens	German	Merciful, mild.
Kliment	Russian	Merciful, mild.
Knox	Irish Gaelic	From the Hillod.
Knut	Old Norse	A knot. The name of several Danish kings.
Kolet	Aboriginal	A dove.
Kolos	Hungarian	Scholar.
Kolya	Aboriginal	Winter. Also a Russian nickname from Nikolai (see Nicholas).
Konan	Irish Gaelic	Wise and intelligent.
Konol	Aboriginal	The sky.
Konrad	German/Polish	German and Polish form of Conrad. Bold, wise counselor.
Konstantin	German/Russian/Scandinavian	Steadfast.
Kont	Hungarian	
Kontar	Ghanese	Only child.
Koora	Aboriginal	The day.
Koorong	Aboriginal	A canoe.
Korey	Celtic/Gaelic	Dweller in the hollow. A boy or girl's name.
Kornel	Czech/Polish	A horn.
Korvin	Latin	Crow.
Kosmo	Greek	Perfect order, harmony.
Kostya	Russian	Steadfast.
Kovan		
Kozma	Greek	Decoration.
Kripa	Hindu	Has a twin sister Kripi.
Kris	Greek	A follower of Christ, a Christian. A boy or girl's name.
Krischnan	Greek	Christian.
Krishna	Sanskrit	Dark, black.
Krispen	Latin	The curly-haired one.
Krispin	Latin	The curly-haired one.

Kristen	Danish	A follower of Christ, a Christian. A boy or girl's name.
Kristian	Swedish	A follower of Christ. A Christian.
Kristoffer	Scandinavian	Bearing Christ. The patron saint of travelers. Also see Christian.
Krunal	Hindu	
Kulan	Aboriginal	A possum.
Kuldeep	Hindu	
Kulvir	Hindu	
Kumar	Sanskrit	A boy or son.
Kunal	Hindu	
Kund	Hungarian	a name of a honor
Kupe	Polynesian	The name of a heroic explorer.
Kurt	German	A bold counselor.
Kuruk	Native American	A bear.
Kusagra	Hindu	a king
Kush	Hindu	son of Rama
Kushan	Hindu	
Kwan	Korean	Strong.
Kyle	Scottish Gaelic	From the narrow strait. Also the name of a Scottish region.
Kyler	Dutch	archer
Kynan	Irish Gaelic	Wise and intelligent.
Kyne	Old English	Royal.
Kyran	Irish	Dark, black.
Laban	Hebrew	White.
Label	Hebrew	lion
Laborc	Hungarian	brave panther
Lachlan	Scottish Gaelic	From the land of the lochs.
Lacy	Old French	Lace.
Ladd	English	A page or attendant.
Ladislav	Slavonic	A glorious ruler, or glorious power. Also see Vladislav.
Ladomar	Hungarian	Trapper.
Lae	Laos	dark
Laertes	Greek	A legendary figure.

Lafayette	French	Faith.
Lafeu		From Shakespeare's play All's Well that Ends Well.
Lai	Sanskrit	The beloved one.
Laibrook	Old English	The path by the brook.
Laidley	Old English	From the water meadow.
Laird	Scottish Gaelic	Head of household.
Lakota	Native American	Friend.
Lakshman	Sanskrit	Auspicious.
Lakshya	Hindu	Target.
Lalit	Hindu	
Lam	Vietnamese	Full understanding; knowledge.
Laman	happy, content	
Lamar	Teutonic	Famous around the land.
Lambert	Teutonic	From the bright or famous land.
Lamberto	Latin	Wealthy in land, brilliant.
Lamech	Hebrew	Strong or powerful.
Lamont	Old Norse/French	Old Norse: A lawyer. French: The mount.
Lance	Old French	A lance bearer. Also see Lancelot.
Lancelot	Old French/Old English	A spear or lance attendant. The most famous of King Arthur's knights.
Lander	Middle English, Greek	Property owner, lion man.
Landers	Old French	A launderer.
Landon	Old English	From the long hill.
Lane	Old English	From the narrow road. A boy or girl's name.
Lang	Teutonic	A tall man.
Langford	Old English	From the long ford.
Langley	Old English	From the long meadow.
Langston	Old English	The farm of the tall man.
Langworth	Old English	From the long enclosure.
Lani	Polynesian	The sky. A boy or girl's name.
Lann	Celtic	A sword.
Lanny	Old English	From the rocky land.

Lantos	Hungarian	Lute player.
Lanyon	Cornish	A cold pool or lake.
Laoghaire	Irish	calf herder, a Shepard.
Laris	Latin	Cheerful.
Larrie	Latin	From the Laurel tree or crowned with laurels. Nickname of Laurence.
Larry	Latin	From the Laurel tree or crowned with laurels. Nickname of Laurence.
Lars	Scandinavian	Scandinavian form of Laurence. From the Laurel tree or crowned with laurels.
Larson	Scandinavian	The son of Lars. From the Laurel tree or crowned with laurels. Also see Laurence.
Lartius		From Shakespeare's play Coriolanus.
Lascelles	Old French	The hermitage or cell.
Lasse	Finnish	Finnish form of Laurence.
Laszlo	Hungarian	Hungarian form of Ladislav. A glorious ruler, or glorious power.
Latham	Old Norse	A division.
Latif	Arabic	Kind and gentle.
Latimer	Old French	An interpreter or teacher.
Lauchlan	Scottish Gaelic	From the land of the lochs.
Laughlin	Scottish Gaelic	From the land of the lochs.
Launce	Old French	A lance bearer. Also see Lancelot.
Launcelot	Old French/Old English	A spear or lance attendant.
Laurence	Latin	From the Laurel tree or crowned with laurels.
Laurie	Latin	From the Laurel tree or crowned with laurels.
Lavache		From Shakespeare's play All's Well that Ends Well.
Lawford	Old English	From the ford by the hill.
Lawler	Irish Gaelic	The mumbler, the soft-spoken one.
Lawley	Old English	From the meadow on the hill.

Lawrance	Latin	From the Laurel tree or crowned with laurels.
Lawrence	Latin	From the Laurel tree or crowned with laurels.
Lawson	Old English	The son of Lawrence or Laurence. From the Laurel tree or crowned with laurels.
Lawton	Old English	From the town on the hill.
Laxman	Sanskrit	Auspicious.
Layland	Greek	Protector of men. From the name Alexander, but also an independent name.
Layton	Old English	The dweller at the farm by the meadow.
Lazarus	Hebrew	God is my help. The man who Jesus raised from the dead in the Bible.
Leal	Old English	Loyal and true.
Leander	Greek	The lion man. The name of a hero in Greek legend. Also see Leo, Leonard and Lionel.
Lear	Teutonic	Joyful, or from the sea.
LeBeau		From Shakespeare's play As You Like It.
Lech	Polish	The name of the legendary founder of Poland.
Lee	Old English	A meadow or clearing. A boy or girl's name.
Lehel	Hungarian	breathes
Leif	Old Norse	Beloved, or a descendant, an heir.
Leigh	Old English	A meadow or clearing. A boy or girl's name.
Leighton	Old English	The dweller at the farm by the meadow.
Leith	Scottish Gaelic	A broad river. A Scottish location.
Lel	Hungarian	Bugler.
Leland	Old English	From the meadowland.
Lemuel	Hebrew	Devoted to God.

Len	Scottish Gaelic	From a Scottish district and a surname. From the name Lennox, Leonard, etc. Len is sometimes used as an independent name.
Lennie	Scottish Gaelic	From a Scottish district and a surname. From the name Lennox, Leonard, etc.
Lennon	Irish Gaelic	A little cape or cloak.
Lennox	Scottish Gaelic	From a Scottish district and a surname.
Lenny	Scottish Gaelic	From a Scottish district and a surname. From the name Lennox, Leonard, etc.
Lensar	English	With his parents.
Leo	Latin	A lion, lion-hearted. Also see Leander, Leonard, Leopold and Lionel.
Leon	Latin	A lion, lion-hearted. Also see Leander, Leonard, Leopold and Lionel.
Leonard	Germanic	As brave as a lion. Also see Leander, Lionel and Leo.
Leonardo	Italian/Portuguese/Spanish	As brave as a lion. Also see Leander, Lionel and Leo.
Leonato		From Shakespeare's play Much Ado About Nothing.
Leonidas	Greek	One who is bold as a lion.
Leonine		From Shakespeare's play Pericles.
Leontes		A character in William Shakespeare's Winter's Tale.
Leopold	Teutonic	Brave for the people, patriotic. The name of kings of Belgium and Bohemia.
Leron	Arabic	The song is mine.
Leroy	French	The king. Also see Elroy.
Leshem	Hebrew	Precious stone.
Lesley	Scottish Gaelic	From an ancient surname. A boy or girl's name.

Leslie	Scottish Gaelic	Meadowlands.
Lesta	Russian	Lestie
Lester	Old English	From the location Leicester, meaning a Roman site or fort.
Lev	Russian	A lion, lion-hearted. Also see Leander, Leonard, Leopold and Lionel.
Levent	Turkish	
Levente	Hungarian	Being.
Leverett	Old French	A young hare, rabbit.
Leverton	Old English	From the farm of the rushes.
Levi	Hebrew	United.
Levin	Latin	A lion, lion-hearted. Also see Leander, Leonard, Leopold and Lionel.
Lewie	Teutonic	A famous warrior. From the name Aloysius, Lewis and Louis.
Lewis		An English variation of Louis. Also an anglicized form of the Welsh name Llewellyn.
Lex	Greek	Protector of men. From the name Alexander, but also an independent name.
Leyman	Old English	A man from the meadow or valley.
Li	Chinese	Strength.
Liall	Old French	From the island.
Liam	Irish Gaelic	Determined guardian.
Lief	Old Norse	Beloved, or a descendant, an heir.
Lincoln	Old English	The settlement at the lake or pool.
Lind	Old English	From the hill of the Lime trees.
Lindan	Old English	From the hill of the Lime trees.
Lindberg	Teutonic	The hill of the Lime trees.
Lindell	Old English	From the valley of Lime trees.
Linden	Old English	From the hill of the Lime trees.
Lindley	Old English	From the Lime tree meadow. A boy or girl's name.
Lindsay	Scottish	From an old Scottish clan surname.

Linford	Old English	From the Lime tree ford.
Linley	Old English	From the field of Flax. A boy or girl's name.
Linton	Old English	From the Flax farm or enclosure.
Linus	Greek	Flaxen-haired.
Linwood	Old English	Stream forest.
Lionel	Old French	A young lion. Also see Leander, Leo and Leonard.
Lipet	Hungarian	Brave.
Lisle	French	From the island.
Litton	Old English	From the place on the river.
Livingston	Old English	A dear friend's place.
Ljluka	Sanskrit	An owl.
Llewellyn	Welsh	Lion-like, a leader or ruler.
Llfryn	Welsh	An uncommon Welsh name.
Lloyd	Welsh	Grey-haired.
Lobsang	Tibetan/Sherpa	The kind-hearted one.
Loch	Scottish Gaelic	A lake.
Locke	Old English	From the stronghold.
Lockwood	Old English	From the enclosed wood.
Lodovico		From Shakespeare's play Othello.
Logan	Scottish Gaelic	Small cove.
Lokesh	Hindu	
Loman	Irish Gaelic	Enlightened. The name of several early Irish saints.
Lombard	Latin	Long-bearded.
Lome	English/Scottish	From a location in Scotland. Also see Laurence.
Lon		From the name the names Alphonso and Laurence.
London	English	Fierce ruler of the world.
Longaville		From Shakespeare's play Love's Labour's Lost.
Lonnie		Handsome one.
Lorand	Hungarian	Brave warrior.
Lorant	Hungarian	A form of Roland.

Loren	Latin	From the Laurel tree or crowned with laurels. A boy or girl's name.
Lorenz	German	From the Laurel tree or crowned with laurels.
Lorenzo	Italian	From the Laurel tree or crowned with laurels.
Lorimer	Old French	A harness and spur-maker.
Lorin	Latin	From the Laurel tree or crowned with laurels.
Lorinc	Hungarian	Laurentian
Loring	Teutonic	A man from Lorraine, a former French province (now part of Alsace-Lorraine).
Lorne	Celtic	Of Lorne.
Lothair	Teutonic/Old French	Teutonic: A famous warrior. Old French: A lute player.
Lothar	German	A famous warrior.
Lothario	Italian	A famous warrior.
Loughlin	Scottish Gaelic	From the land of the lochs.
Louis	Teutonic	A famous warrior. A name borne by sixteen French kings. Also see Lewis.
Lovel	Old French	A little wolf.
Lovell	Old French	A little wolf.
Lowan	Aboriginal	A male fowl. A boy or girl's name.
Lowell	Old French	A little wolf.
Loxley	Old English	The place of a lock of hair.
Loyal	Old French	True, faithful.
Luc	French	A man from Lucania.
Lucas	Greek	A man from Lucania.
Lucentio		From Shakespeare's play Taming of the Shrew.
Lucian	Latin	Person of Light. A boy or girl's name.
Lucilius	Latin	Light. Also see Luke.
Lucio	Italian/Spanish	Light. Also see Luke.
Lucius		From Shakespeare's play Julius Caesar, Timon of Athens and Titus Andronicus.

Lucretius	Latin	Gain. An early Roman poet.
Lucullus		From Shakespeare's play Timon of Athens.
Ludlow	Old English	From the prince's hill.
Ludovic	Scottish	An English variation of Louis.
Ludvig	Scandinavian	A famous warrior.
Ludwig	German	A famous warrior.
Ludwik	Polish	A famous warrior.
Luigi	Italian	A famous warrior.
Luis	Portuguese/Spanish	A famous warrior.
Luke	Greek	A man from Lucania. One of Christ's apostles, and the author of the third book of the New Testament. Also see Lucian.
Lundy	French	Born on Monday. Also the name of an island off the coast of England.
Lunt	Old Norse	From the sacred wood.
Luther	Teutonic/Old French	Teutonic: A famous warrior. Old French: A lute player.
Luzio	Italian	Light. Also see Luke.
Lykaios	Greek	Wolfish, of a wolf, wolf-like.
Lyle	Old French	From the island.
Lyman	Old English	A man from the meadow or valley.
Lymoges		From Shakespeare's play King John.
Lyn	Welsh	Good looking. A boy or girl's name.
Lyndell	Old English	From the valley of Lime trees.
Lyndon	Old English	From the hill of the Lime trees.
Lynn	Old English/Welsh	Old English: A waterfall. Welsh: Good looking. A boy or girl's name.
Lyonel	Old French	A young lion. Also see Leander, Leo and Leonard.
Lyre	Old English	A fork from river or glen.
Lysander	Greek	The liberator. A boy or girl's name.
Lysimachus		From Shakespeare's play Pericles.
Lytton	Old English	From the place on the river.

Maaka	Maori	Maori form of Mark. From Marcus, which relates to Mars, the God of war.
Maarten	Dutch	Don't deceive.
Mablevi	African	do not deceive
Mabon	Welsh	A son.
Mac	Scottish	The son of. Diminutive of names beginning with `Mac'.
Macarius	Latin	Blessed.
Macbeth		From Shakespeare's play Macbeth.
Macdonald	Scottish Gaelic	The son of Donald. The ruler of the world.
Macduff		From Shakespeare's play Macbeth.
Mace	Latin	Aromatic spice, incense.
Macey	Old English	Little Matthew. A man.
Mackay	Gaelic	Son of the fiery one.
Mackenzie	Scottish Gaelic	The son of the handsome one.
Macmorris		From Shakespeare's play Henry V.
Macon	Middle English	To make.
Macy	Old French, Old English	From Matthew's land, club.
Madan	Hindu	
Maddock	Old Welsh	Champion, good fortune.
Maddox		Son of the patron.
Madhav	Hindu	Krishna.
Madhusudhana	Hindu	Krishna.
Madison	Old English	Child of Maud or Matthew. A boy or girl's name.
Madoc	Old Welsh	Fortunate.
Madron	Latin	A nobleman. A Jewish name. Also a Cornish location.
Magee	Scottish Gaelic	The son of the handsome one.
Magne	Norse	Fierce warrior.
Magnus	Latin	The great one.
Magus	Greek	A magician or priest.

Mahabala	Hindu	Strength.
Mahavira	Hindu	Son of Priyavrata.
Mahendra	Sanskrit	The great God Indra (the God of the sky).
Mahesh	Sanskrit	A great ruler.
Mahir	Hebrew	Industrious.
Mahmood	Arabic	Praiseworthy. Also see Muhammad.
Mahomet	Arabic	The praised one. Also see Mahmood.
Mahon	Irish	A bear.
Maitland	Old French	From the meadowland.
Maitreya	Hindu	Disciple of sage Parasara.
Majid	Arabic	The illustrious one.
Major	Latin	Greater.
Maka	Aboriginal	A small fire.
Makani	Hawaiian	The wind. A boy or girl's name.
Makepeace	Old English	Peace maker.
Makis	Greek	Greek form of Michael.
Mako		The name of a shark.
Maksim	Russian	The greatest.
Makya	Native American	The eagle hunter.
Mal		A follower of St. Columba, 'the dove'. From the name Malcolm, Malden and other names.
Malachi	Hebrew	The messenger of the Lord. A prophet in the Bible.
Malcolm	Scottish Gaelic	A follower of St Columba, `the dove'.
Malcom	Scottish	Disciple of Saint Columbia
Malden	Old English	From the hill with a monument.
Malik	Arabic	The master or king.
Malin	Old English	A little warrior.
Malise	Scottish Gaelic	The servant of God. A boy or girl's name.
Mallee	Aboriginal	Scrubland.
Mallory	Old French	Unlucky. A boy or girl's name.
Malone	Irish Gaelic	A devotee of St John.
Malvern	Old Welsh	The bare hill.

Malvolio		From Shakespeare's play Twelfth Night.
Mamillius		From Shakespeare's play Winter's Tale
Mamoru	Japanese	Earth.
Manavendra	Hindu	
Manchu	Chinese	Pure.
Manco	Peruvian	King.
Mandek	Polish	Army man, soldier.
Mandel	Teutonic/Jewish	Teutonic: An almond. Jewish: A little man.
Mander	English	From me.
Mandhatri	Hindu	Prince.
Mandu	Aboriginal	The sun.
Manfield	Old English	From the communal field.
Manfred	Teutonic	A man of peace.
Mani	Aboriginal/Sanskrit	Aboriginal: Equal. Sanskrit: A jewel. A boy or girl's name.
Manik	Hindu	
Manish	Hindu	
Manley	Middle English	Brave and manly.
Mannie	Hebrew	God is with us.
Manning	Old English	Son of Man.
Mannix	Irish Gaelic	A little monk.
Manny	Hebrew	God is with us.
Manoj	Hindu	
Mansa	African	A king.
Mansoor	Arabic	Victorious.
Mansukh	Hindu	
Mansur	Arabic	Divinely aided.
Manu	Polynesian	The man of the birds.
Manuel	Spanish	God is with us.
Manus	Irish	The great one.
Marama	Polynesian	The moon man.
Marc	French	Warlike.

Marcade		From Shakespeare's play Love's Labour's Lost.
Marcel	Latin	From Marcus, which relates to Mars, the God of war. Also see Marius and Martin.
Marcell		From Marcus, which relates to Mars, the God of war. Also see Marius and Martin.
Marcello	Italian	From Marcus, which relates to Mars, the God of war. Also see Marius and Martin.
Marcellus	French	From Marcus, which relates to Mars, the God of war. Also see Marius and Martin.
Marcin	Polish	warlike
Marco	Italian/Spanish	From Marcus, which relates to Mars, the God of war. Also see Marius and Martin.
Marcos	Portuguese	From Marcus, which relates to Mars, the God of war. Also see Marius and Martin.
Marcus	Latin	From Marcus, which relates to Mars, the God of war. Also see Marius and Martin.
Marden	Old English	from the valley with the pool
Mardian		From Shakespeare's play Antony & Cleopatra.
Margarelon		From Shakespeare's play Troilus & Cressida.
Marian	French/Polish	Bitter, as in a bitterly wanted child. Also - The star of the sea. A boy or girl's name.
Marijan	Slowenian	Marian.
Marino	Latin	Of the sea. Masculine form of Marina.
Mario	Latin	Virile. The warlike one. From a Roman family name. Also see Mark and Martin.

Marion	Old French from Latin	Bitter, as in a bitterly wanted child. Also - The star of the sea. A boy or girl's name.
Marius	Latin	Virile. The warlike one. From a Roman family name. Also see Mark and martin.
Mark	Latin	From Marcus, which relates to Mars, the God of war. Also see Marius and Martin.
Markandeya	Hindu	A sage.
Marland	Old English	From the lake land.
Marley	Old English	From the pleasant meadow.
Marlon	Old French	Wild falcon. A boy or girl's name.
Marlow	Old English	From the lake or pond.
Marmaduke	Irish	The servant of Madoc.
Marmion	French	The tiny one.
Maron	Greek	A character from Greek mythology.
Marot	Hungarian	Moravian.
Marron	Aboriginal	A leaf.
Marsden	Old English	From the valley boundary.
Marsh	Old English	From the marshy land.
Marshall	Teutonic	A horse-keeper, or a steward.
Marston	Old English	The place by the marsh.
Martin	Latin	Of Mars, the Roman God of war. Also see Marius and Mark.
Martius		From Shakespeare's play Titus Andronicus.
Marty		Of Mars, the Roman God of war. Also see Marius and Mark.
Marvin	Old English	Friend of the sea.
Marvyn	Old English	A famous friend.
Masa	Japanese	Good and straightforward. A boy or girl's name.
Masakazu	Japanese	First son of Masa.
Maslin	Old French	Little twin.
Mason	Old French	A stone mason.
Massimo	Italian	The greatest.

Masud	Arabic	The fortunate one.
Matai	Hebrew	Gift of God.
Matanga	Hindu	Sage, adviser to Devi Lalita.
Matareka	Polynesian	The one with a smiling face.
Matari	Aboriginal	A man.
Mather	Old English	Strong army.
Matt		A gift of God. Also see Macey and Madison.
Matthew	Hebrew	A gift of God. One of the twelve apostles and the author of the first book of the New Testament. Also see Macey and Madison.
Maui	Polynesian	A legendary hero. The name of a Hawaiian island.
Maurice	Latin	Dark-skinned, like a Moor. Also see Morrison.
Mawgan	Cornish	The name of a saint.
Max		From the stream of Magnus.
Maxey	Old English	From the island of Magnus.
Maximilian	Latin	The greatest.
Maxwell	Scottish Gaelic	From the stream of Magnus.
Mayer	Hebrew	One who gives light.
Maynard	Teutonic	Powerful, brave.
Mayon	Hindu	The black God.
Mead	Old English	From the meadow.
Meara	Gaelic	Merry.
Mearann	Aboriginal	To call.
Mecaenus		From Shakespeare's play Antony & Cleopatra.
Medord	Hungarian	Great, strong.
Medwin	Old English	A friend from the meadow.
Megyer	Hungarian	Hungarian.
Mehetabel	Hebrew	Favored by God, God is doing good.
Mehul	Hindu	A derivative of Mukul.
Meir	Hebrew	One who gives light.

Meirion	Welsh	A traditional name of uncertain meaning.
Meka	Hawaiian	Eyes.
Mel	Old French	From the bad or poor settlement. From the name Melville, Melvin, etc. Also used as an independent name.
Melancton	Greek	Black flower.
Melbourne	Old English	From the millstream.
Melburn	Old English	From the millstream.
Melchior	Persian	The king of the city.
Melford	Old English	From the ford by the hill.
Melik	Turkish	
Melor	Celtic	A Cornish location.
Melrose	Old English	From the bare moor.
Melun		From Shakespeare's play King John.
Melville	Old French	From the bad or poor settlement.
Melvin	Old French	Mill worker.
Melvyn	Old French	From the bad or poor settlement.
Menachem	Hebrew	The comforter.
Menadue	Cornish	From the dark hill.
Menas		From Shakespeare's play Antony & Cleopatra.
Mendel	Hebrew	The comforter.
Menecrates		From Shakespeare's play Antony & Cleopatra.
Menelaus		From Shakespeare's play Troilus & Cressida.
Menenius		From Shakespeare's play Coriolanus.
Menteith		From Shakespeare's play Macbeth.
Menyhart	Hungarian	Royal light.
Mercade		From Shakespeare's play Love's Labour's Lost.
Mercer	Old French	A merchant.
Mercutio		From Shakespeare's play Romeo & Juliet.
Meredith	Old Welsh	A lord. A boy or girl's name.

Merle	Old French	A blackbird. A boy or girl's name.
Merlin	Old Welsh	From the fort by the sea, or the falcon. Also a boy's name (Merlin). A boy or girl's name.
Merrick	Welsh	Welsh form of Maurice. Dark-skinned, like a Moor.
Merrill	Old English	Of the bright sea. Also joyful, happy. A boy or girl's name.
Merryn	Cornish	The name of a saint and a village. A boy or girl's name.
Mert	Turkish	
Merten	German	Of Mars, the Roman God of war. Also see Marius and Mark.
Merton	Old English	The place by the lake.
Merv		Friend of the sea.
Mervin		Friend of the sea.
Mervyn	Old English	A famous friend.
Messala		From Shakespeare's play Julius Caesar.
Mete	Turkish	
Meyer	Hebrew	One who gives light.
Mica	Latin	The name of a mineral.
Micah	Hebrew	A Hebrew form of Michael, mentioned in the Bible.
Michael	Hebrew	Like the Lord. One of the archangels in the Bible.
Michelangelo	Italian from Hebrew	Michael the angel. The first name of the famous artist Michelangelo Buonarroti.
Mick	Hebrew	Like the Lord.
Mickey	Hebrew	Like the Lord.
Midas	Greek	A legendary figure that transformed all that he touched into gold.
Miguel	Portuguese/Spanish	Like the Lord.
Mihaly	Hebrew	Who is like God?
Mihir	Hindu	
Mikael	Swedish	Like the Lord.

Mike	Hebrew	Like the Lord.
Mikhail	Russian	Like the Lord.
Miki	Aboriginal/Japanese	Aboriginal: The moon. Japanese: A stem. A boy or girl's name.
Mikkel	Danish	Like the Lord.
Mikkeli	Hebrew	Like the Lord.
Mikko	Finnish	Like the Lord.
Miklos	Czech	Czech form of Nicholas.
Miko	Finish	
Miksa	Hungarian	Similar to God.
Milan	Czech	The favored or beloved one. Also see Milos.
Milbourn	Old English	From the millstream.
Milburn	Old English	From the millstream.
Miles	Latin/Teutonic	Latin: A soldier. Teutonic: Merciful.
Milford	Old English	From the ford by the mill. A Welsh and New Zealand location
Milind	Hindu	
Millard	Old English	The mill-keeper.
Miller	Old English	A miller.
Milo	Latin/Teutonic	Latin: A soldier. Teutonic: Merciful.
Milos	Czech	Favored Also see Milan.
Milton	Old English	From the mill town.
Minar	Aboriginal	A mariner.
Minas	Scottish Gaelic	The great one.
Miner	Latin	Youth.
Minesh	Hindu	
Ming	Chinese	After a dynasty.
Mingma	Tibetan/Sherpa	Born on a Tuesday.
Minos	Greek	The son of Zeus in Greek mythology.
Miro	Aboriginal	A throwing stick.
Miroslav	Slavonic	Great glory.
Mischa	Hebrew	Like the Lord.
Mitali	Hindu	Friend.
Mitch		Like the Lord.

Mitcham	Old English	The large homestead.
Mitchel	Hebrew	Like the Lord.
Mitchell	Old English	Like the Lord.
Mitesh	Hindu	
Mladen	Slavic	Forever in youth.
Moffatt	Scottish Gaelic	From the long plain.
Mog	high Lord	
Mogens	Danish	The great one.
Mogo	Aboriginal	A stone axe.
Mohammed	Arabic	The praised one. Also see Mahmood.
Mohan	Sanskrit	The bewitching one.
Mohin	Hindu	
Mohinder	Sanskrit	The great God Indra (the God of the sky).
Mohit	Hindu	
Molloy	Irish Gaelic	A venerable chieftain.
Monro	Irish Gaelic	From the mouth of the River Roe, in Ireland.
Monroe	Irish Gaelic	From the mouth of the River Roe, in Ireland.
Montague	Old French	Sharp cliff.
Montana		The name of an American State.
Montano		From Shakespeare's play Othello.
Monte		Sharp cliff.
Montego		Mountainous.
Montgomery	Old French	From the hill of the powerful man.
Monti	Aboriginal	A stork.
Montmorency	Old French	From the hill of Maurentius.
Monty		Sharp cliff.
Mopsa		From Shakespeare's play Winter's Tale
Mor	Hungarian	Moorish.
Moray	Scottish Gaelic	From the land by the sea. Derived from the region of Moray.
Morcum	Cornish	From the valley near the sea.

Mordecai	Babylonian Or Hebrew	A Biblical name.
Mordred	Teutonic	Brave counsel. An Arthurian knight.
Morgan	Welsh	The bright sea. A boy or girl's name.
Moriarty	Irish	Sea warrior.
Morice	Latin	Dark-skinned, like a Moor. Also see Morrison.
Moritz	German	Dark-skinned, like a Moor. Also see Morrison.
Morland	Old English	From the moors.
Morley	Old English	From the clearing on the moor.
Morrell	Latin	Dark-skinned, like a Moor. Also see Morrison.
Morrie	Latin	Dark-skinned, like a Moor. Also see Morrison.
Morris	Latin	Dark-skinned, like a Moor. Also see Morrison.
Morrison	Old English	The son of Maurice. Dark-skinned, like a Moor.
Morry	Latin	Dark-skinned, like a Moor. Also see Morrison.
Morse	Latin	Dark-skinned, like a Moor. Also see Morrison.
Mort	Middle English	Stumpy. Also from the name Mortimer and Morton.
Morten	Danish	Of Mars, the Roman God of war. Also see Marius and Mark.
Mortimer	Old French	Lives near the sea.
Morton	Old English	From the town near the moor.
Morty		Lives near the sea.
Morven	Gaelic	A Scottish region. A boy or girl's name.
Moses	Egyptian	Drawn out of the water.
Moshe	Jewish	Drawn out of the water.
Mosi	Swahili	The firstborn.

Moss	Egyptian	Probably meaning born of the Biblical patriarch who led the Israelites out of Egypt (Moses).
Mostyn	Welsh	From the field of the fortress.
Motega	Native American	New arrow.
Moth		From Shakespeare's play Midsummer-Night's Dream and Love's Labour's Lost.
Mountjoy		From Shakespeare's play Henry V.
Mowan	Aboriginal	The sun.
Mubarak	Arabic	Blessed. Fortunate.
Muhammad	Arabic	The praised one. Also see Mahmood.
Muir	Scottish	The moor.
Mukasa	Ugandan	God's chief administrator.
Mukhtar	Arabic	The chosen one.
Mukta	Hindu	Means a pearl in Telugu.
Mukul	Hindu	
Mukunda	Hindu	
Mulga	Aboriginal	An Acacia tree.
Mull	Middle English	Grinder.
Mullion	Aboriginal	An eagle. Also a Cornish location.
Mumtaz	Arabic	
Mungo	Scottish Gaelic	A dear friend.
Munro	Irish Gaelic	From the mouth of the River Roe, in Ireland.
Murdoch	Scottish Gaelic	A mariner.
Murdock	Scottish	victorious at sea
Murphy	Irish Gaelic	A warrior of the sea. A boy or girl's name.
Murray	Scottish Gaelic	From the land by the sea. Derived from the region of Moray.
Musa		An Arabic form of Moses.
Mustafa	Arabic	The chosen one.
Mustardseed		From Shakespeare's play Midsummer-Night's Dream.

Mutius		From Shakespeare's play Titus Andronicus.
Muzaffer	Turkish	
Myall	Aboriginal	Wild and an Acacia tree. Also a form of Michael.
Myer	Hebrew	One who gives light.
Myles	Latin/Teutonic	Latin: A soldier. Tuetonic: Merciful.
Mylo	Latin/Teutonic	Latin: A soldier. Tuetonic: Merciful.
Mylor	Celtic	A Cornish location.
Myron	Greek	Fragrant. From myrrh, an aromatic shrub. A boy or girl's name.
Naaman	Hebrew	Pleasant.
Nabendu	Hindu	
Nabil	Arabic	Noble.
Nabulung	African	Do not receive.
Nachiketa	Hindu	Nachik.
Nachmanke	Hebrew	compassionate one, one who comforts
Nadav	Hebrew	nobel, a generous one
Nadir	Arabic	Precious, rare.
Naeem	North African	Benevolent.
Nahum	Hebrew	The comforter.
Naimish	Hindu	
Nairn	Scottish Gaelic	The dweller by the Alder tree. A location.
Nakul	Hindu	
Nalong	Aboriginal	The source of the river.
Nalren	Dene Indian	Thawed out.
Nambur	Aboriginal	A tea-tree.
Namdev	Hindu	Poet, saint.
Namid	Native American	A dancer.
Namir	Hebrew	Like a leopard.
Nanda	Sanskrit	Joy.
Nandin	Hindu	The delightful, follower of Shiva.
Nandor	Hungarian	
Nantan	Apache Indian	Spokesman.
Napoleon	Greek	Fierce one from Naples.

Narayan	Sanskrit	The son of man.
Narayana	Hindu	Vishnu.
Narciso	Latin	A lily, daffodil.
Narcissus	Greek	The flower. Also the name of the youth in Greek mythology who fell in love with his own reflection.
Nardu	Aboriginal	A plant with edible seeds.
Narendra	Sanskrit	The mighty man.
Naresh	Hindu	
Narrah	Aboriginal	The sea.
Narsi	Hindu	Poet, saint.
Nartana	Hindu	Makes others dance.
Nash	Old English	Cliff.
Nasir	Arabic	The helper, the supporter.
Nassir	Arabic	Protector.
Nat		The gift of God. A Biblical prophet.
Natal	Spanish	Christmas.
Natale	Old French	Christmas.
Natan	Aboriginal	A fig tree.
Nathan	Hebrew	The gift of God. A Biblical prophet.
Nathaniel		Gift of God.
Naum	Russian	The comforter.
Naveen	Hindu	Navin.
Nawang	Tibetan/Sherpa	The possessive one.
Nayan	Hindu	
Neal	Irish Gaelic	The champion. Also see Nelson.
Neale	Irish Gaelic	The champion. Also see Nelson.
Ned	Old English	A rich guardian.
Neddie	Old English	A rich guardian.
Neddy	Old English	A rich guardian.
Nedim	Turkish	
Neel	Hindu	Blue.
Neeraj	Hindu	
Nehemiah	Hebrew	The consolation of the Lord.
Neil	Irish Gaelic	Champion.

117

Neill	Irish Gaelic	The champion. Also see Nelson.
Nek	Italian	
Nelek	Polish	Like a horn.
Nelson	English	The son of Neal or Neil. The champion.
Nemo	Latin	No name, nobody.
Neo	Greek	New.
Nerang	Aboriginal	Little.
Nerhim	Turkish	
Nero	Latin	Dark, or black-haired.
Neron	Spanish	Strong, stern.
Nesim	Turkish	
Nesip	Turkish	
Nestor	Greek	Wisdom.
Nevada	Spanish	Snow, or as white as snow. Also the name of an American state. A boy or girl's name.
Nevan	Irish	Holy, little saint.
Neville	Old French	From the new town or settlement.
Nevin	Irish Gaelic	The servant of the saints.
Newbold	Old English	From the new building.
Newell	Old English	From the new hall.
Newlyn	Celtic	The dweller at the new pool. A boy or girl's name.
Newman		New comer.
Newton	Old English	From the new town or estate.
Niall	Irish Gaelic	The champion. Also see Nelson.
Nic	Latin	Belonging to the Lord. St Dominic founded an important order of monks.
Nicholas	Greek	The victory of the people.
Nick	Latin	Belonging to the Lord.
Nickie	Latin	Belonging to the Lord. See Dominic.
Nickson	Old English	The son of Nicholas. The victory of the people.
Nicky	Latin	Belonging to the Lord.
Nico	Italian	The victory of the people.

Nicodemus	Greek	victory of the people
Nicol	Scottish	The victory of the people.
Nicolas	Spanish	The victory of the people.
Nieander	Greek	A man of victory.
Niel		The gift of God. From the name Nathan.
Niels	Latin	A horn.
Nieodemus	Greek	The conqueror for the people.
Nigel	Latin	Dark, black-haired.
Nihar	Hindu	Mist, fog, dew.
Nike	Greek	Victory.
Nikhil	Hindu	
Nikita	Russian/Greek	Unconquered people. A boy or girl's name.
Niklaus	Scandinavian	The victory of the people.
Nikunj	Hindu	
Nilay	Hindu	
Nils	Norwegian/Swedish	The victory of the people.
Nilson	English	The son of Neal or Neil. The champion. Also from the famous British admiral, Lord Nelson.
Nima	Tibetan/Sherpa	Sun. A boy or girl's name.
Nimai	Hindu	Name of Lord Krishna.
Nimbus	Latin	Rain cloud, halo.
Nimesh	Hindu	
Nimrod	Hebrew	Valiant, or great hunter.
Ninian	Gaelic	The name of a 5th century saint.
Nino	Italian	God is gracious. From the name Gianni and Giovanni.
Nioka	Aboriginal	Green hills.
Niraj	Hindu	Lotus flower.
Niramitra	Hindu	Son of Pandava Sahadeva.
Niran	Thai	Eternal.
Niranjan	Hindu	
Nirav	Hindu	
Nirel	Hebrew	God's field.

Nishad	Hindu	The musical note Ni.
Nishan	Armenian	A sign.
Nisi	Hebrew	Emblem, symbol.
Nitesh	Hindu	
Niven	Irish Gaelic	The servant of the saints.
Nivens	Irish Gaelic	The servant of the saints.
Nixon	Old English	The son of Nicholas. The victory of the people.
Noadiah	Hebrew	God assembles
Noah	Hebrew	Rest, peace.
Noam	Hebrew	Pleasant.
Noble	Latin	Famous, noble.
Nodin	Native American	Wind.
Noe	Spanish	Peace, rest.
Noel	Old French	Christmas.
Noi	Laos	Small, little.
Nolan	Irish Gaelic	Famous, a champion.
Norbert	Teutonic	Light or brilliance from the North.
Norbu	Tibetan/Sherpa	A precious gem.
Norm		Norseman or ruler.
Norman	Teutonic	Norseman or ruler.
Normand		Norseman or ruler.
Norris		Norseman or ruler.
North	Old English	From the North.
Northclif	Old English	From the north cliff.
Northrop	Old English	From the Northern farm.
Norton	Old English	From the Northern farm or town.
Norville	Old English	From the Northern farm or town.
Norvin	Old English	A friend from the north.
Norwell	Old English	From the north spring or well.
Norwood	Old English	From the Northern forest. Also a guard at the North gate.
Nowell	Old French	Christmas.
Nowra	Aboriginal	A black cockatoo. A town in NSW.
Nuncio	Italian	A messenger.

Nur	Hebrew	Fire.
Nurhan	Turkish	
Nuri	Arabic	Fire.
Nye	Welsh	Truly golden.
Nyek	Hungarian	Borderlands.
Nyle	Old English	Island.
Nym		From Shakespeare's play Henry V and Merry Wives of Windsor.
Oakes	Middle English	The dweller by the Oak trees.
Oakley	Middle English	One who lives at the Oak tree meadow.
Obadiah	Hebrew	The servant of God.
Obelix	Greek	Pillar of strength. From Egyptian obelisk.
Oberon		A character in William Shakespeare's A Midsummer Night's Dream.
Obert	Teutonic	Wealthy and bright.
Obiajulu	African	The heart is consoled.
Ochen	Ugandan	One of the twins.
Octavius	Latin	The eighth born.
Oddvar	Norse	The spear's point.
Odell	Old Norse	Wealthy.
Odern	Aboriginal	By the sea.
Odil	French	Rich.
Odin	Old Norse	The Scandinavian God of war.
Odion	Nigerian	First born twin.
Odolf	Teutonic	A noble wolf.
Odon	Hungarian	Wealthy protector.
Odysseus	Greek	Full of wrath, wrathful.
Ogden	Old English	From the valley of Oak trees.
Ogilvie	Celtic	From the high hill.
Ogilvy	Old Scottish	from the high peak
Oglesby	Old English	Awe-inspiring.
Oguz	Hungarian	Arrow.
Okan	Turkish	

Okely	Middle English	One who lives at the Oak tree meadow.
Okko	Finnish	From the name Oscar.
Olaf	Old Norse/Scandinavian	Ancestor.
Olcay	Turkish	
Oldrich	Czech	One with riches and power.
Oleg	Russian	The name of an early prince of Kiev.
Oleos	Spanish	Holy oil used in church.
Olier	Breton	
Olin	Old English	Holly.
Oliver	Latin	An Olive tree or branch. A symbol of peace.
Olivier		From Shakespeare's play As You Like It.
Ollie		An Olive tree or branch. A symbol of peace.
Omar	Arabic	First born son.
Omarjeet	Hindu	
Ompoly	Hungarian	Enough.
Ond	Hungarian	Tenth child.
Onslow	Old English	The hill of the zealous one.
Onur	Turkish	
Ora	Latin/Polynesian	Latin: Light, golden. Polynesian: Life. A boy or girl's name.
Orad	Aboriginal	Earth.
Oram	Old English	From the enclosure by the riverbank.
Oran	Irish Gaelic	Pale-skinned.
Orazio	Italian	From a Roman family name.
Orban	Hungarian	A city dweller.
Ordway	Old English	The spear fighter.
Orelious	Roman	After Marcus Aurelius.
Oren	Hebrew	A tree. Also see Oran.
Orestes	Greek	A man of the mountain. A hero of Greek mythology.
Orfeo	Italian	A name from ancient mythology.

Orford	Old English	A dweller at the ford.
Orion	Greek	The son of light. The name of a constellation.
Orlan	Old English	From the pointed land. A boy or girl's name.
Orlando	Italian	Italian form of Roland. Famed throughout the land. The name of Shakespeare's hero in As You Like It.
Orman	Old English	A spearman.
Ormond	Old English	A spearman.
Ormos	Hungarian	Like a cliff.
Oroiti	Polynesian	The slow-footed one.
Orpheus	Greek	A name from ancient mythology.
Orran	Irish Gaelic	Pale-skinned.
Orren	Irish Gaelic	Pale-skinned.
Orrin	Irish Gaelic	Pale-skinned.
Orsen	Old French from Latin	A little bear.
Orsino		A little bear.
Orson	Old French from Latin	A little bear.
Orton	Old English	From the farm by the river.
Orville	Old French	Golden city.
Orvin	Old English	A spear friend.
Osaze	Hebrew	Favored by God.
Osbert	Old English	Divinely bright or famous.
Osborn	Old English	A divine warrior.
Osborne	Hebrew	Soldier of God.
Oscar	Old English	A divine spearman.
Osgood	Old Norse	A pagan god.
Osip	Russian	God shall add.
Oskar	German	A divine spearman.
Oskari	Finnish	A divine spearman.
Osman	Arabic	An Ottoman Turk, or a servant of God.
Osmar	Old English	Divinely glorious.

Osmond	Old English	A divine protector.
Osric	Old English	A divine ruler.
Ossian	Latin	Fawn, young deer.
Oswald	Old English	Divinely powerful.
Oswin	Old English	A friend of God, or a divine friend.
Oszlar	Hungarian	
Otello	Italian	Rich, prosperous.
Othello	Italian	Prosperous.
Otis	Greek	Keen of hearing.
Ottavio	Italian	The eighth born.
Otto	Teutonic	Rich, prosperous.
Otway	Teutonic	Fortunate in battle.
Ove	Scandinavian	A well-known Scandinavian name.
Ovid	Latin	Lamb.
Owen	Welsh	Well-born. Also a Welsh form of John (see Evan).
Oxford	Old English	From the ford of the oxen. An English university city.
Oxton	Old English	From the ox enclosure.
Oz	Hebrew	Strength.
Ozan	Turkish	
Ozaner	Turkish	
Ozias	Old English	From the ox enclosure.
Ozor	Hungarian	Name of an ethnic group.
Ozsvot	Hungarian	Deity, might, strength.
Paavo	Finnish	Finnish form of Paul.
Pablo	Spanish	Small. Spanish form of Paul.
Pacifico	Spanish from Latin	Peaceful.
Packard	Old English	One who packs.
Paco	Native American	Gold eagle. Also a Spanish nickname of Francis.
Paddy	Latin	Noble, well born. From the name Patrick.
Padget	French	A young attendant or page.
Padgett	French	A young attendant or page.
Padmakar	Hindu	

Padraig	Irish Gaelic	Noble, well born.
Padruig	Scottish Gaelic	Noble, well born.
Page	French	A young attendant or page. A boy or girl's name.
Pahniro	Latin	Born on Palm Sunday.
Paige	Old English/French	A young child. French: A young attendant or page. A boy or girl's name.
Paine	Old French	A countryman.
Paki	Egyptian	A witness.
Palani	Hawaiian	A free man.
Pallav	Hindu	
Palmer	Old English	A palm-bearing pilgrim.
Palti	Hebrew	My escape.
Pan		The Greek God of nature.
Pancho	Spanish	Tuft, plume.
Pancras	Greek	All-powerful. The name of an early saint.
Pancrazio	Italian	Supreme ruler, all powerful.
Pandarus		From Shakespeare's play Troilus & Cressida.
Pandita	Hindu	Scholar.
Pandya	Hindu	
Pankaj	Hindu	Lotus flower.
Panos	Greek	A rock.
Panthino		From Shakespeare's play Two Gentlemen of Verona.
Panyin	Ghanese	Eldest of twins.
Paolo	Italian	Italian form of Paul. Small.
Parag	Hindu	
Paramartha	Hindu	Great entity.
Paras	Hindu	Touchstone.
Paris	Greek	A character in Greek mythology.
Park	Old English	From the park.
Parker	Old English	The park keeper.
Parkin	Old English	Little Peter. A stone or rock.

Parlan	Gaelic	Plowman, farmer.
Parolles		From Shakespeare's play All's Well that Ends Well.
Parr	Old English	A dweller by the cattle pen.
Parri	Aboriginal	A stream.
Parrish	Old English	From the church parish.
Parry	Welsh	The son of Harry. Army power, or ruler of the army.
Parsefal	Old French	To pierce the valley.
Parsifal	Old French	To pierce the valley.
Parth	Hindu	A name given to Arjuna by Lord Krishna
Partha	Hindu	A name given to Arjuna by Lord Krishna
Pasang	Tibetan/Sherpa	Born on a Friday. A boy or girl's name.
Pascal	Latin	Born at Easter.
Pat	Latin	Nobleman. The name of the patron saint of Ireland.
Patamon	Native American	Raging.
Patern	Breton	
Patony	Hungarian	
Patrick	Latin	Nobleman. The name of the patron saint of Ireland.
Patroclus		From Shakespeare's play Troilus & Cressida.
Patton	Old English	A warrior.
Paul	Latin	Small. Also see Pollock.
Paulo	African	Place of rest.
Pavel	Polish/Russian/Swedish	Small. Also see Pollock.
Pax	Latin	Peace.
Paxton	Old English	From the estate of the warrior.
Payton	Old English	A dweller on the warrior's farm.
Pazman	Hungarian	Right, man.
Peace	Latin	Peace.

Pearce	Greek	A stone or rock. Also see Ferris, Parkin and Pierson.
Peder	Greek	Stone.
Pedr	Welsh	A stone or rock. Also see Ferris, Parkin and Pierson.
Pedrek	Cornish/Welsh	The name of a famous Celtic saint (Petroc).
Pedro	Spanish	A stone or rock. Also see Ferris, Parkin and Pierson.
Pedrog	Cornish/Welsh	The name of a famous Celtic saint (Petroc).
Pelin	Turkish	
Pell	Old English	A scarf.
Pellegrin	Hungarian	Pilgrim.
Pelton	Old English	From the farm by a pool.
Pemba	Tibetan/Sherpa	Born on a Saturday.
Pembroke	Celtic	A broken hill.
Penley	Old English	From the enclosed meadow.
Penn	Old English	An enclosure or pen.
Penrice	Cornish	From the end of the ford.
Penrith	Welsh	The chief ford.
Penrod	Teutonic	A famous commander.
Penrose	Cornish/Welsh	The end or top of the moor.
Pentele	Hungarian	Merciful, lion.
Penwyn	Welsh	The fair-haired one.
Pepe	Spanish	God shall add.
Pepin	Teutonic	The petitioner, one who seeks a favor.
Pepper	English	From the pepper plant.
Per	Scandinavian	Scandinavian form of Peter. A stone or rock.
Percival	Old French	To pierce the valley.
Percy	Norman	A Norman surname from a location. Also from the name Percival.
Peregrine	Latin	A stranger or pilgrim. Also a type of falcon.
Pericles		From Shakespeare's play Pericles.

Peril	Latin	A trial or test.
Perri	English	Wanderer.
Perry	Old English/French	The dweller by the pear tree. Also from the name Peregrine. A boy or girl's name.
Perth	Celtic	A thornbush thicket. Also cities in Scotland and Western Australia.
Pete		A rock.
Peter	Greek	A stone or rock. One of Christ's apostles.
Petroc	Cornish/Welsh	The name of a famous Celtic saint.
Petruchio		From Shakespeare's play Taming of the Shrew.
Peverall	French	A piper.
Phelan	Irish Gaelic	As brave as a wolf.
Phelps	Old English	The son of Philip. A lover of horses.
Philario		A lover of horses. Also see Phelps and Phillips.
Philbert	Teutonic	Very bright.
Philemon	Greek	Loving.
Philip	Greek	A lover of horses. One of the new testament apostles. Also see Phelps and Phillips.
Phillip		A lover of horses. One of the new testament apostles. Also see Phelps and Phillips.
Phillips	Old English	The son of Philip. A lover of horses.
Philo	Greek	Loving.
Philostrate		From Shakespeare's play Midsummer-Night's Dream.
Philotus		From Shakespeare's play Timon of Athens.
Phineas	Egyptian/Hebrew	Egyptian: The Nubian (dark-skinned). Hebrew: An oracle.
Phoenix	Greek	The legendary bird that rose again from its own ashes. A boy or girl's name.
Phuoc	Vietnamese	Good luck.

Phuong	Vietnamese	Destiny.
Picerious	Greek/Latin	From the word Pi.
Pickford	Old English	From the ford at the peak.
Pierce	Greek	A stone or rock. Also see Ferris, Parkin and Pierson.
Piero	Italian	A stone or rock. Also see Ferris, Parkin and Pierson.
Pierpont	French	A stone bridge.
Pierre	French	A stone or rock. Also see Ferris, Parkin and Pierson.
Pierrot	French	A stone or rock. Also see Ferris, Parkin and Pierson.
Piers	Greek	A stone or rock. Also see Ferris, Parkin and Pierson.
Pierson	English	The son of Peter. A stone or rock.
Piet	Dutch	A stone or rock. Also see Ferris, Parkin and Pierson.
Pietro	Italian	A stone or rock. Also see Ferris, Parkin and Pierson.
Pilan	Native American	supreme essence
Pinch		From Shakespeare's play Comedy of Errors.
Pindan	Aboriginal	A desert.
Pindari	Aboriginal	From the high ground.
Pindarus		From Shakespeare's play Julius Caesar.
Pino	Italian	A lover of horses. From the name names such as Filippo. See Philip.
Pip		From the name Philip.
Piran	Cornish	A saint's name.
Pisanio		From Shakespeare's play Cymbeline.
Pistol		From Shakespeare's play Henry V and Merry Wives of Windsor.
Pita	Maori	Maori form of Peter. A stone or rock.
Pitney	Old English	Preserving one's island.
Pitt	Old English	From the hollow.

Pius	Latin	Pious, devout. The name of several Popes.
Piusz	Hungarian	Pious, Pius
Piyush	Hindu	
Placido	Latin	Calm, quiet.
Plato	Greek	Strong shoulders.
Platon	Greek	Broad-shouldered.
Platt	Old French	From the flat land or plateau.
Pluto	Greek	The mythological God of the underworld.
Pol	Irish Gaelic	Small. Also see Pollock.
Polixenes		From Shakespeare's play Winter's Tale.
Pollock	Old English	Little Paul. Small.
Polonius		From Shakespeare's play Hamlet.
Pomeroy	French	From the apple orchard.
Pompey		From Shakespeare's play Measure for Measure.
Pongor	Hungarian	All might.
Pontius	Latin	The fifth.
Porter	French	The gatekeeper.
Powell	Welsh	The son of Howell. The eminent one.
Powys	Welsh	A man from Powys, a Welsh county.
Prabhakar	Hindu	Cause of luster, shine.
Prabodh	Hindu	
Pradeep	Hindu	Light.
Praful	Hindu	
Prakash	Sanskrit	Light, or famous.
Pramana	Indonesian	Wisdom.
Pramath	Hindu	
Pramsu	Hindu	A scholar.
Pranav	Hindu	Ohm.
Pranay	Hindu	Love, romance.
Prasad	Sanskrit	Brightness.
Prasanth	Hindu	
Prasata	Hindu	Father of Draupad.

Prashant	Hindu	
Prasoon	Hindu	
Prassana	Hindu	Cheerful.
Pratap	Hindu	
Pratik	Hindu	Symbol.
Pratyush	Hindu	
Praveen	Hindu	Proficient.
Prayag	Hindu	
Preetish	Hindu	
Prem	Sanskrit	Love.
Prentice	Old English	Beginner, learning.
Prescott	Old English	Priest's cottage.
Presley	Old English	From the priest's meadow.
Preston	Old English	From the priest's farm or town.
Prewitt	Old French	Valiant one.
Priam	Greek	A mythological king of Troy.
Price	Welsh	The son of the loving man.
Primel	Breton	See also Primael, Privel.
Primo	Latin	The firstborn son.
Prince	Latin	The first in rank.
Prior	Latin	The head of a monastery or priory.
Prithu	Hindu	First Ksatriya, son of Vena.
Privrata	Hindu	Son of Satarupa.
Probert	Welsh	The son of Robert. Famous, bright fame.
Proctor	Latin	The administrator or manager.
Proculeius		From Shakespeare's play Antony & Cleopatra.
Prometheus	Greek	Forethought.
Prosper	Latin	Fortunate. Prosperous.
Prospero		From Shakespeare's play The Tempest.
Proteus	Greek	Changeable.
Pryce	Welsh	The son of the loving man.
Pryderi	Welsh	To care for.

Pryor	Latin	The head of a monastery or priory.
Ptolemy	Greek	Mathematician.
Publius		From Shakespeare's play Julius Caesar and Titus Andronicus.
Puck		From Shakespeare's play Midsummer-Night's Dream.
Pulkit	Hindu	
Pundarik	Hindu	White in color.
Puranjay	Hindu	
Purujit	Hindu	Conqueror of many.
Purvis	Old French	The purveyor, provider.
Pusan	Hindu	A sage.
Puskara	Hindu	
Putnam	Old English	From the sire's estate.
Qasim	Arabic	One who shares or distributes.
Quasim	Arabic	One who divides goods among his people.
Quemby	Old Norse	From the woman's estate.
Quennel	French	The one who lives at the little Oak tree.
Quentin	Latin	The fifth, as in the fifth-born child. A boy or girl's name.
Quigley	Irish Gaelic	A spinning distaff.
Quillan	Irish Gaelic	A cub.
Quilliam	Gaelic	Gaelic form of William. A strong and resolute protector.
Quimby	Old Norse	From the woman's estate.
Quinby	Scandinavian	From the queen's estate.
Quince		From Shakespeare's play Midsummer-Night's Dream.
Quincy	Latin/French	The fifth, as in fifth child. A boy or girl's name.
Quinlan	Irish Gaelic	Well-shaped, athletic.
Quinn	Irish Gaelic	Wise and intelligent. A boy or girl's name.
Quinney	Gaelic	The son of the crafty one.
Quintin	Latin	The fifth, as in the fifth-born child.
Quinton	Latin	The fifth, as in the fifth-born child.
Quintus	Latin	Fifth, as in the fifth child.
Quirce	Spanish	The name of a 4th-century martyr.

Quirino	Spanish	The name of a 4th-century martyr.
Rab	Scottish	Scottish nickname for Robert. Famous, bright fame.
Rabbie	Scottish	Scottish nickname for Robert. Famous, bright fame.
Rad	Old English	A counselor. Also a diminutive of names beginning with `rad'.
Radborne	Old English	From the red brook or stream.
Radcliff	Old English	Red cliff.
Radcliffe	Old English	From the red cliff.
Radek	Czech	Glad.
Radford	Old English	From the red ford.
Radley	Old English	From the red meadow.
Radman	Slavic	Joy.
Radnor	Old English	From the red shore.
Radom	Hungarian	Happy, peace.
Raeburn	Teutonic	Dweller by the stream where does drink.
Rafael	German/Portuguese/Spanish	God heals, or healed by God.
Rafe		An alternative form and pronunciation of Ralph.
Raffaele	Italian	God heals, or healed by God.
Rafferty	Irish Gaelic	Prosperous.
Rafi	Arabic	The exalted one.
Rafiq	Arabic	A companion, a friend.
Rafu	Japanese	A net.
Raghnall	Irish	A wise and powerful ruler. Also see Reginald, Reynold and Ronson.
Ragin	Hindu	
Ragnar	Scandinavian	A wise warrior.
Rahman	Arabic	Merciful.
Rahul	Hindu	
Raibeart	Scottish	Scottish Gaelic form of Robert. Famous, bright fame.
Raidon	Japanese	Thunder God.

Raimy	Raimee	
Rainer	German	A wise warrior.
Rainier	French	A wise warrior.
Raivata	Hindu	A Manu.
Raj	Sanskrit	A king.
Rajan	Hindu	
Rajanikant	Hindu	
Rajendra	Sanskrit	A mighty king.
Rajesh	Hindu	
Rajiv	Sanskrit	Striped.
Rakesh	Hindu	
Raleigh	Old English	The meadow of the Roe deer.
Ralph	Old English	Wolf counselor. A fearless adviser. Also see Rolf and Rudolph.
Ralston	Old English	A dweller on Ralph's farm or estate.
Ram	Hindu	Lord Rama.
Raman	Hindu	
Ramanuja	Hindu	A saint.
Rambert	Teutonic	Mighty and brilliant.
Rambures		From Shakespeare's play Henry V.
Ramelan	Indonesian	A prophecy.
Rameses	Egyptian	Born of the sun.
Ramesh	Sanskrit	Ruler of Rama.
Ramiro	Spanish	A great judge or adviser.
Ramon	Spanish	A wise or mighty protector.
Ramsay	Old English	An island of wild garlic. Most commonly used in Scotland.
Ramsden	Old English	The ram's valley.
Ramsey	Old English	Ram's land.
Ranald	Old English	A wise and powerful ruler. Also see Reginald, Reynold and Ronson.
Rance	French	A kind of Belgian marble.
Rand		A wolf-like shield. From the name Randolph.
Randal	Old English	A wolf-like shield.
Randall	Old English	A wolf-like shield.

Randell	Old English	A wolf-like shield.
Randie		A wolf-like shield or the admired one. A boy or girl's name.
Randolph	Old English	A wolf-like shield.
Randy		A wolf-like shield or the admired one. A boy or girl's name.
Ranen	Hebrew	joyous
Ranger	Old French	The keeper of the forest.
Rangi	Maori/Polynesian	Heaven or the sky. A boy or girl's name.
Ranjan	Hindu	
Ranjeet	Hindu	
Ranjit	Sanskrit	The delighted one.
Rankin	Old English	A little shield.
Ransford	Old English	From the ford of the raven.
Ransley	Old English	From the meadow of the Raven.
Ransom	Old English	A warrior's son.
Rantidev	Hindu	devotee of Narayana
Ranulf	Old Norse	Wolf-like advice.
Raoul	French	French form of Ralph.
Raphael	Hebrew	God has healed. One of the four archangels in the Bible.
Rarna	Sanskrit	Pleasing. An alternative name for the Hindu God Vishnu.
Rashid	Arabic	The well guided one a director.
Rashne	Persian	Judge, arbitrator
Rasmus	Greek	Worthy of love.
Rastus	Greek	The loving one.
Rata	Aboriginal/Polynesian	Aboriginal: A plant. Polynesian: The name of a great chief. A boy or girl's name.
Ratri	Hindu	Night.
Rauf	Arabic	The compassionate one.
Raul	Italian	The counsel of the wolf. A fearless adviser. Also see Rolf and Rudolph.
Raven	Old English	A raven.

Ravi	Sanskrit	Of the sun.
Ravid	Hebrew	The wanderer.
Ravindra	Hindu	
Ravinger	Old English	Ravine.
Rawiri	Maori	Maori form of David. The beloved, the adored one.
Rawley	Old English	From the meadow of the Roe deer.
Rawlins	Old English	Son of a little wise wolf.
Rawly	Old English	From the meadow of the Roe deer.
Rawson	Old English	The son of the little wolf.
Ray	Old French	A stream or a king. A boy or girl's name.
Rayburn	Old English	From the deer brook.
Raymon	Teutonic	A wise or mighty protector.
Raymond	Teutonic	Wise protection.
Raynard	Teutonic	Brave, or a fox.
Rayner	German	A wise warrior.
Raynold	Old English	A wise and powerful ruler. Also see Reginald and Ronald.
Razi	African	secret
Read	Old English	Red-haired.
Reading	Old English	Son of the redheaded one.
Reagan		Wise.
Rearden	Irish Gaelic	A royal poet.
Reardon	Irish Gaelic	A royal poet.
Rebel	Latin	The rebellious one. A boy or girl's name.
Redford	Old English	From the red ford.
Redman	Old English	A protector, an adviser.
Redmond	Irish	A wise or mighty protector.
Redmund	Teutonic	A wise or mighty protector.
Reece	Welsh	Ardent.
Reed	Old English	Red-haired.
Reede	Old English	Red-haired.
Rees	Welsh	Ardent.
Reese	Welsh	Ardent one.

Reeve	Old English	A steward.
Regan	Irish Gaelic	The descendant of a king. A boy or girl's name.
Regin	Old Norse	A figure from mythology.
Reginald	Old English	A wise and powerful ruler. Also see Reynold and Ronald.
Regis	French	Ruler, king.
Rego	Hungarian	
Rehan	Arabic	
Reid	Old English	Red-haired.
Reilly	Irish Gaelic/Old English	Irish Gaelic: Valiant. Old English: A Rye meadow.
Reinhard	German	Brave, or a fox.
Reinhold	German	A wise and powerful ruler. Also see Reginald and Ronald.
Remington	Old English	From the farm of ravens.
Remus	Latin	Fast. In legend, one of the brothers who founded Rome.
Remy	French from Latin	An oarsman.
Renaldo	Spanish	A wise and powerful ruler. Also see Reginald, Reynold and Ronson.
Renard	Teutonic	Brave, or a fox.
Renaud	French	Brave, or a fox.
Rendor	Hungarian	Policeman.
Rene	Latin	Reborn. A boy or girl's name.
Renfred	Old English	Mighty but peaceful.
Renfrew	Celtic	From the still river.
Rennard	Teutonic	Brave, or a fox.
Renny	Irish Gaelic	Small but powerful. A boy or girl's name.
Renshaw	Old English	From the forest of the Ravens.
Reuben	Hebrew	Behold a son. One of Jacob's sons in the Bible.
Reuel	Hebrew	Friend of God.
Rex	Latin	A king. Also see Ray and Roy.

Rey	Old French	A king. Also see Raymond, Rex and Roy.
Reynaldo		From Shakespeare's play Hamlet.
Reynard	Teutonic	Brave, or a fox.
Reynold	Old English	A wise and powerful ruler. Also see Reginald and Ronald.
Rezse	Hungarian	
Rhett	English	Possibly a form of Rhys, but most likely invented for Margaret Mitchell's character, Rhett Butler, in Gone with the Wind.
Rhisiart	Welsh	Brave and strong.
Rhodes	Greek	The place of roses. The name of an Aegean island.
Rhodri	Welsh	The ruler of the wheel.
Rhun	Welsh	Grand.
Rhydwyn	Welsh	A dweller by the white ford.
Rhys	Welsh	Ardent.
Rian	Irish Gaelic	A little king.
Ric	Old Norse	Honorable ruler. From the name Eric and Richard.
Richard	Teutonic	Brave and strong.
Richman	Old English	A powerful protector.
Rick		Brave and strong. From the name Eric and Richard.
Ricker	Old English	A powerful army.
Rico	Spanish	Noble ruler.
Rider	Old English	A horseman or knight.
Ridgeway	Old English	From the ridge road.
Ridgley	Old English	From the meadow's ridge.
Ridley	Old English	From the cleared wood.
Rigby	Old English	The valley of the ruler.
Rigg	Old English	From the ridge.
Rikard	Scandinavian	Brave and strong.
Rikin	Hindu	

Riley	Irish Gaelic/Old English	Irish Gaelic: Valiant. Old English: A Rye meadow. A boy or girl's name.
Rimon	Arabic	Pomegranate.
Rinaldo	Italian	A wise and powerful ruler. Also see Reginald, Reynold and Ronson.
Ring	Old English	A ring.
Ringo	Old English	A bell-ringer.
Rinzen	Tibetan/Sherpa	The holder of intellect. A boy or girl's name.
Riordan	Irish Gaelic	A royal poet.
Ripley	Old English	From the shouter's meadow.
Rishab	Hindu	The musical note Re.
Rishi	Hindu	
Rishley	Old English	From the wild meadow.
Rishon	Hebrew	First.
Risley	Old English	From the brushwood meadow.
Riston	Old English	From the brushwood farm.
Ritchell	Vietnamese	Nasty, gross.
Ritchie	Teutonic	Brave and strong.
Ritter	Teutonic	A knight.
Rivers	Latin, French	Stream of water.
Rizal	Philippino	Rizzy.
Roald	Old Norse	A famous ruler. A Norwegian form of Ronald.
Roan	Irish Gaelic	Little red-haired one.
Roarke	Irish Gaelic	A famed ruler.
Rob		Famous, bright fame.
Robert	Teutonic	Famous, bright fame.
Robertson		The son of Robert. Famous, bright fame.
Robi	Hungarian	Shining with fame.
Robin	English	A small bird. A boy or girl's name.
Robinson	English	The son of Robert or Robin. Famous, bright fame.
Robyn	English	A small bird. A boy or girl's name.
Rocco	Teutonic	To rest.

Rochester	Old English	A rocky fortress, or camp on the rocks.
Rock	Old English	From the rock.
Rockley	Old English	From the rocky meadow.
Rockwell	Old English	From the rocky well or spring.
Rocky	Teutonic	To rest.
Rod	Teutonic	A renowned ruler.
Rodd		A renowned ruler.
Roddie	Teutonic	A renowned ruler.
Roddy	Teutonic	A renowned ruler.
Roden	Old English	From the valley of the reeds. A boy or girl's name.
Roderick	Teutonic	A renowned ruler.
Roderigo	Italian/Spanish	A renowned ruler.
Rodman	Teutonic	A famous hero.
Rodney	English	Land near the water.
Rodolf	Duch/German	A famous wolf. Also see Ralph and Rolf.
Rodolfo	Italian/Spanish	A famous wolf. Also see Ralph and Rolf.
Rodrigo	Italian/Spanish	A renowned ruler.
Rodrigue	French	A renowned ruler.
Rodwell	Old English	From the Christian's well.
Rogan	Irish Gaelic	The red-haired one.
Rogelio	Spanish	Beautiful one.
Roger	Teutonic	A famous spearman or warrior.
Rohan	Sanskrit	Little red-haired one.
Rohit	Hindu	Red color.
Rokus	Hungarian	
Roland	Teutonic	Famed throughout the land.
Roldan	English	Powerful, mighty.
Rolf	Teutonic	The famous wolf. Also see Ralph and Rudolph.
Rollo	Teutonic	From the famed land.
Roly	Old English	From the rough meadow.
Roman	Latin	A citizen of Rome.

Romeo	Latin	A pilgrim to Rome. A famous Shakespearean character.
Romney	Welsh	A curving river. A location in Kent, England.
Romulus	Latin	One of the legendary brothers who founded Rome.
Ronak	Hindu	
Ronald	Old English	A wise and powerful ruler. Also see Reginald, Reynold and Ronson.
Ronan	Irish Gaelic	Little seal. A boy or girl's name.
Rongo	Maori/Polynesian	The God of rain and fertility.
Roni	Hebrew	My joy.
Ronin	Japanese	Samurai without a master.
Ronit	Hebrew/Irish Gaelic	Hebrew: A song. Irish Gaelic: Prosperity.
Ronson	Old English	The son of Ronald. A wise and powerful ruler.
Rooney	Irish Gaelic	Red-haired.
Roosevelt	Dutch	Field of roses.
Roper	Old English	A rope maker.
Rory	Irish Gaelic	The red king. A boy or girl's name.
Roscoe	Old Norse	From the Deer forest.
Rosencrantz		From Shakespeare's play Hamlet.
Roshan	Persian	Splendid. One who emanates light. A boy or girl's name.
Roslin	Old French	The small red-haired one.
Ross	Scottish Gaelic	Woody meadow.
Roswald	Teutonic	A mighty horse.
Roth	German	Red-haired.
Rothwell	Old Norse	From the red well or spring.
Rourke	Irish Gaelic	A famed ruler.
Routledge	Old English	From the red pool.
Rowell	Old English	From the deer spring.
Rowland	Teutonic	From the famed land.
Rowley	Old English	From the rough meadow.
Rowse	Cornish	From the heathland.

Rowson	Old English	The son of the red-haired man.
Roxbury	Old English	From the rock fortress.
Roy	Old French/Scottish Gaelic	Old French: A king. Scottish Gaelic: The red one. From the name Royce.
Royce	Old English	The son of the king.
Roydon	Old English	From the hill of Rye.
Royston	Old English	An English location.
Ruark	Irish Gaelic	A famed ruler.
Ruben	Hebrew	Behold a son. One of Jacob's sons in the Bible.
Rubens	Portuguese	Behold a son. One of Jacob's sons in the Bible.
Rubin	Hebrew	Behold a son. One of Jacob's sons in the Bible.
Ruchir	Hindu	
Rudd	Old English	Of a ruddy complexion.
Rudi	Teutonic	A famous wolf. Also see Ralph and Rolf.
Rudolph	Teutonic	A famous wolf. Also see Ralph and Rolf.
Rudy	Teutonic	A famous wolf. Also see Ralph and Rolf.
Rudyard	Old English	From the red enclosure.
Ruel	Hebrew	Friend of God.
Rufford	Old English	From the rough ford.
Rufus	Latin	Red-haired.
Rugby		From Shakespeare's play Merry Wives of Windsor.
Ruhinda	Caymanian	Prince of Cows.
Rumford	Old English	From the wide ford.
Runako	African	Handsome.
Rune	Old Norse	Secret lore.
Rupert	Teutonic	Famous, bright fame.
Rupesh	Hindu	
Rurik	Russian/Scandinavian	Russian and Scandinavian form of Roderick. A renowned ruler.

Rush	French	Red-haired.
Rushford	Old English	From the ford with rushes.
Ruskin	Teutonic	The small red-haired one.
Russ		Red head. From the name Russell.
Russel	Old French, Old English	Red-haired, fox-like.
Russell	Old French	Red head.
Rusty		Red head. From the name Russell.
Rutger	Dutch	A famous spearman or warrior.
Rutherford	Old English	From the cattle ford.
Rutland	Old Norse	From the stump land.
Rutledge	Old English	From the red pool.
Rutley	Old English	From the stump meadow.
Ry		From the name Rylan and Ryman.
Ryan	Irish Gaelic	A little king.
Rycroft	Old English	From the Rye field.
Ryder	Old English	A horseman or knight.
Rylan	Old English	From the Rye land.
Ryle	Old English	From the hill of Rye.
Ryley	Irish Gaelic/Old English	Irish Gaelic: Valiant. Old English: A Rye meadow.
Rylie	Old English	A small stream.
Ryman	Old English	A rye seller.
Ryoichi	Japanese	First son of Ryo.
Ryozo	Japanese	Third son of Ryo.
Ryton	Old English	From the rye farm.
Ryuichi	Japanese	First son of Ryu.
Saben	Latin	A Sabine man (from central Italy).
Sabir	Arabic	The patient one.
Sabola	Egyptian	Prophetess.
Sabre	French	Sword-like.
Sacha	French	The defender, or helper of mankind. A boy or girl's name.
Sachchit	Hindu	Truth, Consciousness
Sacheverell	Old French	A leap of the young goat.

Sachiel	Hebrew	Angel of water.
Sachin	Hindu	
Sadi	Turkish	
Sadik	Arabic	Truthful, or faithful.
Sadurni	Catalan	
Safak	Turkish	
Safford	Old English	From the willow ford.
Sagar	Hindu	King.
Sage	Old French	Wise. Also the name of a herb. A boy or girl's name.
Sagiv	Hebrew	Mighty, with strength.
Sahadev	Hindu	Prince.
Sahale	Native American	Above.
Sahara		Inca gold.
Sahen	Hindu	Falcon.
Sahib	Hindu	Sir.
Sahnan	Hebrew	Wise and peaceful.
Saidi	African	Helper.
Sakda	Thai	Power.
Sakima	Native American	A king.
Salah	Arabic	Good, righteous.
Salerio		From Shakespeare's play Merchant of Venice.
Salim	Arabic	Safe, secure.
Salisbury	Old English	The fort by the willow pool.
Salman	Arabic	protector, conqueror
Saloman	Hebrew	Peaceful.
Salomo	German	Wise and peaceful.
Salomon	Spanish	Wise and peaceful.
Salter	Old English	A salt seller.
Salton	Old English	From the place in the willows.
Salvador	Spanish from Latin	A savior.
Salvatore	Italian	Savior.
Sam		She who listens also an achievement. A boy or girl's name.

Samien	Arabic	To be heard.
Samir	Hindu	Wind.
Sammie		She who listens also an achievement. A boy or girl's name.
Sammon	Arabic	Grocer.
Sammy		She who listens also an achievement. A boy or girl's name.
Sampath	Hindu	
Sampson	Hebrew	Of the sun, or a strong man. A Biblical name.
Samson	Hebrew	Of the sun, or a strong man. A Biblical name.
Samudra	Hindu	Lord of the ocean.
Samuel	Hebrew	Asked of God. A name from the Bible. Also see Saul.
Sanat	Hindu	
Sanborn	Old English	From the sandy brook.
Sancho	Spanish	Truthful and sincere.
Sandeep	Hindu	Rishi (Sega of Gods), named after Sandipani Rishi
Sanders	Old English	The son of Alexander. Protector of men.
Sandie	Greek	The protector and helper of mankind. A boy or girl's name.
Sandler		
Sandon	Old English	From the sandy hill.
Sandor	Hungarian	Protector of men. From the name Alexander.
Sandy	Greek	The protector and helper of mankind. A boy or girl's name.
Sanford	Old English	From the sandy ford.
Sanjay	Sanskrit	Triumphant.
Sanjeev	Hindu	
Sanjog	Hindu	
Sankara	Sanskrit	Auspicious.
Sansom	Hebrew	Of the sun, or a strong man.
Sansone	Italian	Of the sun, or a strong man.

Santiago	Spanish	Of St James.
Santo	Italian	A saint.
Santon	Old English	From the sandy hill.
Santos	Spanish	Of the saints. Also see Toussaint.
Santosh	Hindu	
Santoso	Indonesian	Peaceful.
Sapan	Hindu	
Sarasvan	Hindu	
Sarat	Hindu	
Sargent	Old French	A military officer.
Sarkis	Armenian	Royalty.
Sarngin	Hindu	Name of God Vishnu.
Sarni	Arabic	The elevated one.
Sarojin	Hindu	Lotus-like.
Sarosh	Persian	Prayer.
Sasha	Russian	The protector and helper of mankind. A boy or girl's name.
Saswata	Hindu	
Satayu	Hindu	Brother of Amavasu and Vivasu.
Satruijt	Hindu	A son of Vatsa.
Saturnino	Latin	Of Saturn, the Roman God of agriculture.
Saturninus		From Shakespeare's play Titus Andronicus.
Satyen	Hindu	
Saudeep	Hindu	
Saul	Hebrew	Asked for, or prayed for. A name from the Bible. Also see Samuel.
Saunak	Hindu	Boy sage.
Saunders	Old English	The son of Alexander. Protector of men.
Saunderson	Old English	The son of Alexander. Protector of men.
Saurabh	Hindu	
Saviero	Italian	Of the new house.
Saville	Old French	From the willow estate.

Sawyer	Old English	A sawer of wood.
Sawyl	Welsh	Welsh form of Saul. Asked for, or prayed for.
Saxby	Old Norse	From the farm of the short sword.
Saxon	Old English	Of the Saxons, or people of the sword. A boy or girl's name.
Saxton	Old English	From the farm of the Saxon.
Sayed	Arabic	The lord, the master.
Sayer	Celtic	A carpenter.
Scarus		From Shakespeare's play Antony & Cleopatra.
Schuyler	Dutch	Shield, scholar.
Scipio	Latin	A staff or walking stick.
Scott	Old English	Of Scottish origin.
Scully	Irish Gaelic	A herald or town crier.
Seabert	Old English	Sea glorious.
Seaborne	Old English	The sea warrior.
Seabrook	Old English	From a brook by the sea.
Sealey	Old English	Blessed.
Seamus	Irish Gaelic	Irish Gaelic form of James. The supplanter.
Sean	Irish Gaelic	Irish Gaelic form of John. God is gracious. Also see Shane.
Seanan	Irish Gaelic	Old, or wise.
Searle	Teutonic	An armed warrior.
Seaton	Old English	A place by the sea.
Sebastian	Latin	Venerable. A man from Sebasta. The name of a 3rd-century saint.
Sebes	Hungarian	Fast, quick.
Secundus	Latin	The second child.
Sedgewick	Old English	From the farm in the rushes.
Sedgley	Old English	From the warrior's meadow.
Seeley	Old English	Blessed.
Seely	Old English	Blessed.
Seff	Hebrew	A wolf.
Sefton	Old English	The dweller at the place in the rushes.

Seger	Old English	The sea warrior.
Seif	Arabic	Sword of religion.
Seiichi	Japanese	First son of Sei.
Selby	Old Norse	From the willow farm.
Seldon	Old English	From the house on the hill.
Seleucus		From Shakespeare's play Antony & Cleopatra.
Selig	Jewish	Blessed fortunate.
Selim	Arabic	Safe, secure.
Selwyn	Latin	Of the woods.
Semih	Turkish	
Sempronius		From Shakespeare's play Timon of Athens and Titus Andronicus.
Semyon	Russian	The listener.
Senach	Gaelic	
Senajit	Hindu	
Senan	Irish Gaelic	Old, or wise.
Sencer	Turkish	
Senichi	Japanese	First son of Sen.
Sennett	Old English	Bold in victory.
Senon	Spanish	Given life by Zeus.
Septimus	Latin	The seventh son.
Serafino	Italian from Hebrew	The ardent one. The masculine form of Seraphina.
Seraphim	Hebrew	Burning ones, angels, ardent.
Serge	Italian	Servant.
Sergeant	Old French	A military officer.
Sergent	Old French	A military officer.
Sergio	Italian	Attendant.
Sergius	Latin	A Roman family name.
Servan	Breton	
Sesto	Latin	The sixth son.
Seth	Hebrew/Sanskrit	Hebrew: A Biblical name meaning the appointed one. One of the sons of Adam and Eve. Sanskrit: A bridge.
Setiawan	Indonesian	Faithful.

Seton	Old English	A place by the sea.
Seung	Korean	Successor, winning.
Sevastian	Russian	A man from Sebasta. The name of a third century saint.
Severin	English	River in England.
Severino	Italian	Severe.
Severn		The name of a British river.
Sevilin	Turkish	Beloved.
Seville	Spanish	A Spanish city.
Seward	Old English	A sea defender.
Sexton	Old French	A church official.
Sextus	Latin	The sixth son.
Seyed	Arabic	The lord, the master.
Seymour	Old French	From a location.
Seyton		From Shakespeare's play Macbeth.
Sezni	Breton	
Shadwell	Old English	From the shady stream.
Shafiq	Arabic	Compassionate.
Shah	Persian	The king.
Shahar	Jewish	The dawn.
Shailen	Hindu	
Shailesh	Hindu	
Shakar	Arabic	Grateful.
Shakir	Arabic	The grateful one.
Shalabh	Hindu	
Shalin	Hindu	
Shallow		From Shakespeare's play Merry Wives of Windsor.
Shalom	Hebrew	Peace. Also see Solomon.
Shaman	Native American	Holy man.
Shamus	Irish Gaelic	Irish Gaelic form of James. The supplanter.
Shanahan	Irish Gaelic	The wise one.
Shandy	Old English	Boisterous.

Shane		From Irish Gaelic a Variation of Sean (John), and so a form of Jane. A boy or girl's name.
Shankar	Sanskrit	He who gives happiness.
Shanley	Irish Gaelic	A venerable hero.
Shannon	Irish	From the name of a river in Ireland. A boy or girl's name.
Shantanu	Hindu	
Sharad	Hindu	
Sharif	Arabic	The honorable one.
Sharma	Sanskrit	Giving protection.
Shashi	Hindu	The moon, moonbeam.
Shashwat	Hindu	Ever lasting.
Shaughan	Irish Gaelic	Irish Gaelic form of John. God is gracious. Also see Shane.
Shaun	Irish Gaelic	Irish Gaelic form of John. God is gracious. Also see Shane.
Shaw	Old English	From the grove of trees.
Shay	Irish Gaelic	The stately one. A boy or girl's name.
Shea	Irish	Hawk-like, stately.
Sheehan	Irish Gaelic	Peaceful.
Sheffield	Old English	From the crooked field, or the sheep field.
Shelby	Old English	The dweller at the ledge estate and a sheltered town. A boy or girl's name.
Sheldon	Old English	From the steep valley.
Shelley	Old English	From the wood, or the meadow's edge. A boy or girl's name.
Shen	Chinese	A deep thinker.
Shepherd	Old English	One who heards sheep.
Sher	Sanskrit	The beloved one or a Lion. A boy or girl's name.
Sherborne	Old English	A clear stream.
Sheridan	Irish Gaelic	The wild one. A boy or girl's name.
Sheridon	Irish	Wild one.
Sherlock	Old English	Fair-haired.

Sherman	Old English	Shearer or servant.
Sherwin	Old English	A swift runner.
Sherwood	Old English	From the bright forest.
Shigekazu	Japanese	First son of Shige.
Shiloh	Hebrew	A place of rest. A Biblical location.
Shima	Japanese	An island dweller.
Shimon	Hebrew	The listener.
Shing	Chinese	Victory.
Shinichi	Japanese	First son of Shin.
Shipley	Old English	From the sheep pasture.
Shipton	Old English	The dweller at the sheep farm.
Shishir	Hindu	
Shiv	Hindu	Lord Shiva.
Shiva	Sanskrit	Benign. An important Hindu God.
Shlomo	Jewish	Wise and peaceful.
Shmuel	Hebrew	Asked of God.
Shoichi	Japanese	First son of Sho.
Sholto	Scottish Gaelic	A sower of seed.
Shomari	Swahili	Forceful.
Shrey	Hindu	
Shuichi	Japanese	First son of Shu.
Shulamith	Hebrew	Peaceful.
Shunichi	Japanese	First son of Shun.
Shunnar	Arabic	Pleasant.
Shvetank	Hindu	
Shyam	Hindu	
Shylock		From Shakespeare's play Merchant of Venice.
Siamak	Persian	Bringer of joy, great emperor.
Siddartha	Sanskrit	One who has accomplished his goal. A name of the Buddha.
Siddel	Old English	From the wide valley.
Siddharth	Hindu	
Sidell	Old English	From the broad valley.

Sidney	Old English/Old French	Old English: From the riverside meadow. Old French: From St Denis.
Siegbert	Teutonic	A famous victory.
Siegfried	Teutonic	Peace after victory.
Sigebryht	Anglo-Saxon	
Sigfried	Teutonic	Victory peace.
Siggy		From the name Siegbert, Siegfried.
Sigi		From the name Siegbert, Siegfried.
Sigmund	Teutonic	A victorious protector.
Sigurd	Old Norse	A victorious guardian.
Silas	Latin	From the forest. Also see Silvester.
Siler	Syler	
Silvanus	Latin	From the forest. Also see Silvester.
Silvester	Latin	Of the woods. Also see Silvanus.
Silvio	Latin	belonging to the forest, silver
Silvius		From Shakespeare's play As You Like It.
Simeon		The Biblical form of Simon.
Similien	Breton	
Simon	Hebrew	The listener. Also see Simpson.
Simonides		From Shakespeare's play Pericles.
Simple		From Shakespeare's play Merry Wives of Windsor.
Simpson		The son of Simon. The listener.
Sinan	Turkish	
Sinbad	Teutonic	A sparkling prince.
Sinclair	French	A clear sign. From St Clair.
Singh	Hindu	Lion.
Sinjon	French	Saint John.
Sinnett	Old English	Bold in victory.
Sinnott	Old English	Bold in victory.
Siva	Sanskrit	Benign.
Sivan	Hebrew	The ninth month.
Siward		From Shakespeare's play MacBeth.
Skeet	Middle English	Speedy.

Skelly	Irish Gaelic	A storyteller.
Skelton	Old English	From the place on the ledge.
Skene	Scottish Gaelic	A bush.
Skipp	Old Norse	Ship owner.
Skipper	Dutch	A ship's captain.
Skjold	Scandinavian	
Sklaer	Breton	See also Sklerijenn.
Slade	Old English	From the valley.
Slate	Middle English	A fine-grained rock.
Slender		From Shakespeare's play Merry Wives of Windsor.
Slevin	Irish Gaelic	The mountain climber.
Sloan	Irish Gaelic	A warrior.
Sly		From the name Silvanus and Silvester.
Smedley	Old English	From the level meadow.
Smith	Old English	A blacksmith.
Snehal	Hindu	
Snorre	Scandinavian	
Snout		From Shakespeare's play Midsummer-Night's Dream.
Snowden	Old English	From the snowy hill.
Snug		From Shakespeare's play Midsummer-Night's Dream.
Socrates		The name of the ancient Greek philosopher.
Sofronio	Greek	Self-controlled
Soham	Hindu	
Sol	Latin	The sun. Also from the name Solomon.
Solan	soul seeker	
Solanio		From Shakespeare's play Merchant of Venice.
Solinus		From Shakespeare's play Comedy of Errors.
Solomon	Hebrew	Wise and peaceful. A son of David in the Bible. Also see Shalom.

Solon	Greek	The wise one.
Solt	Hungarian	Name of an honor.
Solyom	Hungarian	Falcon.
Soma	Hungarian	A kind of berry
Somerled	Old Norse	The summer traveler. A Scottish name.
Somerset	Old English	From the summer farm or settlement. The name of an English county.
Somerville	Old English	From the summery hill.
Sonam	Tibetan/Sherpa	The fortunate one. A boy or girl's name.
Sonnagh	Welsh	mound, rampart
Sonny		Diminutive for names that includes `son'.
Sophocles	Greek	After the classical dramatist.
Soren	Danish from Latin	The stern one.
Sorley	Old Norse	The summer traveler. A Scottish name.
Sorrell	Old French	Bitter. A plant name, and A boy or girl's name.
Soterios	Greek	Savior.
Southwell	Old English	From the southern spring.
Spalding	English	Divided field.
Sparke	Old Norse	The lively one.
Speed		From Shakespeare's play Two Gentlemen of Verona.
Spence		A dispenser of provisions. From the name Spencer.
Spencer	Old French	A dispenser of provisions. Administrator.
Spike	Old English	A nail, or an ear of grain. Generally used as a nickname.
Spiridon	Greek	Of the soul or spirit.
Squire	Old French	A knight's attendant.
Sridhar	Hindu	
Srijan	Hindu	
Srikant	Hindu	

Srinath	Hindu	
Srinivas	Hindu	
Sriram	Hindu	
Stack	Old Norse	A haystacker.
Stacy	Latin	Prosperous or resurrection. A boy or girl's name.
Staffan	Swedish	Swedish form of Stephen. A crown or garland.
Stafford	Old English	From the ford by the landing place.
Stamford	Old English	A dweller at the rocky ford.
Stanbury	Old English	From the stone fort.
Standen	Old English	A dweller in the stony valley.
Standish	Old English	From the rocky pasture.
Stanfield	Old English	From the stony field.
Stanford	Old English	A dweller at the rocky ford.
Stanhope	Old English	From the stony valley.
Stanislaus	Slavonic	The glorious government.
Stanislav		Glory of the camp.
Stanislaw		Glory of the camp. From the name Stanislav.
Stanko	Slovenian	
Stanley	Old English	Rocky meadow.
Stanton	Old English	From the rocky farm or estate.
Stanwick	Old English	From the rocky village.
Starbuck	Old Norse	The stream in the sedges.
Starr	Old English	A star. A boy or girl's name.
Starveling		From Shakespeare's play Midsummer-Night's Dream.
Stavros	Greek	Crowned. Greek form of Stephen.
Stedman	Old English	A farmer.
Steele	Old English	Like steel.
Stefan	German/Polish/Russian/Scandinavian	A crown or garland. Also see Stevenson and Stinson.
Stefanos	Greek	A crown or garland. Also see Stevenson and Stinson.

Steffan	Welsh	A crown or garland. Also see Stevenson and Stinson.
Stein	German	Stone.
Sten	Swedish	A stone.
Stenton	Old English	From the rocky farm or estate.
Stephan	German	A crown or garland. Also see Stevenson and Stinson.
Stephano	Italian	A crown or garland. Also see Stevenson and Stinson.
Stephen	Greek	A crown or garland. Also see Stevenson and Stinson.
Sterling	Old English	A little star, or a starling.
Sterne	Old English	Austere. Stern.
Stert	Old English	From the promontory.
Steve	Greek	A crown or garland. Also see Stevenson and Stinson.
Steven	Greek	A crown or garland. Also see Stevenson and Stinson.
Stevenson		The son of Stephen. A crown or garland.
Stewart	Old English	A steward, or keeper of a household.
Stig	Old Norse	The wanderer.
Stiles	Old English	From the stile.
Stillman		Quiet, gentle.
Stinson	Old English	The son of Stephen, or the son of stone.
Stiofan	Irish Gaelic	Irish Gaelic form of Stephen.
Stockley	Old English	A clearing with tree stumps.
Stockton	Old English	From the place near the tree trunk.
Stoddard	Old English	The horse-keeper.
Stoke	Old English	From the settlement.
Stokley	Old English	From the tree-stump meadow.
Storm	Old English	A tempest. A boy or girl's name.
Storr	Old Norse	A great man.
Stowe	Old English	From the place or religious site.
Stoyan	Bulgarian	to stay

Strahan	Scottish Gaelic	A little valley. A Tasmanian town.
Stratford	Old English	From the ford on a Roman road.
Strato		From Shakespeare's play Julius Caesar.
Stratton	Old English	From the place on a Roman road.
Strom	German, Czech	Stream, tree.
Stroud	Old English	The overgrown marshland.
Stu	Old English	A steward, or keeper of a household.
Stuart	Old English	A steward, or keeper of a household.
Studs	Old English	A house, dwelling.
Sturt	Old English	From the promontory.
Styles	Old English	From the stile.
Subodh	Hindu	
Sudarshan	Hindu	
Sudesha	Hindu	A son of Krishna.
Sudeva	Hindu	Good Deva.
Sudhansu	Hindu	
Sudhir	Hindu	
Sudi	Swahili	Luck.
Suffield	Old English	A dweller in the southern field.
Sugriva	Hindu	
Sukarman	Hindu	Reciter of 1000 Samhitas.
Sukumar	Hindu	Tender.
Sulaiman	North African	Peaceful.
Suleiman	Arabic	Arabic form of Solomon.
Sulio	Breton	
Sullivan	Irish Gaelic	The black-eyed one.
Sully	Gaelic	To stain or dirty.
Sulwyn	Welsh	The fair sun.
Sumadhur	Hindu	Very sweet.
Suman	Sanskrit	Cheerful and wise.
Sumantu	Hindu	Atharva Veda was assigned to him.
Sumati	Hindu	
Sumit	Hindu	
Sumner	Old French	The one who summons.

Sun	Chinese/Korean	Chinese: Bending, or decreasing. Korean: Goodness. A boy or girl's name.
Sundara	Hindu	
Sunil	Hindu	
Surony	Hungarian	Name of an honor.
Suresh	Sanskrit	The ruler of the gods.
Surya	Sanskrit	The sun.
Sutcliffe	Old English	From the south cliff.
Sutherland	Old Norse	From the southern land.
Sutton	Old English	The dweller at the southern farm or town.
Suvrata	Hindu	A child of Daksa.
Svein	Anglo-Saxon	
Sven	Old Norse	A youth.
Swagat	Hindu	
Swain	Old English/Old Norse	Old English: A swineherd. Old Norse: Youthful.
Swapnil	Hindu	
Sweeney	Irish Gaelic	The little hero.
Sweeny	Gaelic	Little hero.
Swindon	Old English	From the hill of the pigs. An English city.
Swinford	Old English	The pig ford.
Swithin	Old English	Strong. The name of an English saint.
Sycamore	Greek	A tree name.
Sydenham	Old English	From the wide river meadow.
Sykes	Old English	At the stream or gully.
Sylvain	French	From the forest. Also see Silvester.
Sylvan	Latin	From the forest. Also see Silvester.
Sylvester	Latin	From the forest, woods.
Symon	Hebrew	The listener.
Synclair		A clear sign.
Syrus	Persian	The name of the founder of the Persian empire. From the name Cyrus.
Szabolcs	Hungarian	

Szalok	Hungarian	
Szemere	Hungarian	Small man, demolisher.
Szervoc	Hungarian	Freed.
Szesco	Hungarian	
Szevor	Hungarian	Serious, strict.
Szilord	Hungarian	
Szolot	Hungarian	
Szymon	Polish	Polish form of Simon. The listener.
Szylve	Scandinavian	
Taavi	Finnish	The beloved, the adored one. From the name David.
Tab	Persian	A drum or drummer.
Tabansi	African	One who endures.
Tabari	North African	After famous Muslim historian.
Tabb	Persian	A drum or drummer.
Tabor	Persian	A drum or drummer.
Tad	Irish Gaelic	A poet or philosopher. Also see Teague.
Tadc	Celtic	
Tadd	Greek	Courageous.
Taddeo	Greek	Courageous.
Tadi	Omaha Indian	Wind.
Taffy	Welsh	The beloved, the adored one. From the name David.
Taggart	Gaelic	A priest.
Tahir	Arabic	Pure and virtuous.
Tai	Vietnamese	The talented one.
Tailer	Old French	The tailor.
Tailor	Old French	The tailor.
Tait	Old Norse	Jolly, cheerful. Also see Tatum.
Tajo	Spanish	Day.
Takai	Japanese	
Takoda	Native American	The friend of all.
Taksa	Hindu	A son of Bharata.
Taksony	Hungarian	Well fed, content, merciless, wild.

Taku	Japanese	
Talbot	Old French	From the valley.
Talfryn	Welsh	From the top of the hill.
Talib	Arabic	
Taliesin	Welsh	A radiant brow.
Tallis	Persian	Wise, learned.
Talman	Hebrew	To injure, to oppress.
Talon		
Talorg	Welsh	
Talos	Greek	Giant protector of Minos island.
Tam	Scottish	A twin or heart. A boy or girl's name.
Tama	Japanese/Polynesian	Japanese: A jewel. Polynesian: A boy or son. A boy or girl's name.
Tamas	Greek	A twin.
Tamer	Turkish	
Tamir	Arabic	Pure, tall, stately.
Tancred	Teutonic	A thoughtful adviser.
Tancredo	Italian	Of thoughtful counsel.
Tane	Polynesian	The name of a god.
Tanek	Polish	Immortal.
Taner	Turkish	
Tangaroa	Polynesian	Of the sea.
Tangwyn	Welsh	Peace.
Tanicus	Latin	
Tannar	Old English	Leather worker.
Tanner	Old English	Leather worker.
Tano	Ghanese	Name of a river.
Tapan	Hindu	
Tapesh	Hindu	
Tara	Irish Gaelic/Sanskrit	Irish Gaelic: A rocky hill, from the ancient home of Ireland's kings. Sanskrit: A star. The name of a Buddhist goddess. A boy or girl's name.
Tarang	Hindu	
Tarasios	Greek	Of Tarentum.

Tarcal	Hungarian	
Tardos	Hungarian	Bald.
Taree	Aboriginal	A wild fig.
Tariq	Arabic	The night visitor.
Tarjan	Hungarian	Name of an honor.
Tarkan	Turkish	
Tarn	Old Norse	A mountain pool.
Taro	Japanese	The firstborn son.
Tarquin	Latin	The name of two early Roman kings.
Tarrant	Old English	From the name of a river.
Tarun	Sanskrit	Young, tender.
Tas	Hungarian	Well fed, stone.
Tashi	Tibetan/Sherpa	Prosperity. A boy or girl's name.
Tate	Old Norse	Jolly, cheerful. Also see Tatum.
Tathal	Welsh	
Tathan	Welsh	
Tatum	Old English	From Tate's homestead. A boy or girl's name.
Taurin	Latin	Born under the sign of Taurus.
Taurinus	Latin	
Taurus		From Shakespeare's play Antony & Cleopatra.
Tavis	Scottish	Twin.
Tavish	Scottish Gaelic	A twin. A form of Thomas.
Tawhiri	Polynesian	A tempest.
Taylor	Old French	A tailor. A boy or girl's name.
Teague	Irish Gaelic	A poet or philosopher.
Teal	English	A water bird. A boy or girl's name.
Tean	Cornish	One of the Isles of Scilly. A boy or girl's name.
Tearlach	Scottish	
Tecer	Turkish	
Tecwyn	Welsh	White, fair.
Ted	Old English	Divine gift.
Teddie	Old English	Divine gift.

Teddy	Old English	Divine gift.
Tee		
Tej	Hindu	
Telford	Old French	An iron-cutter.
Telo	Old French	
Tem	English	Country.
Teman	Hebrew	Right hand, South.
Temani	Hebrew	Of Teman.
Templar	Old French	A knight.
Tenenan	Old French	
Tennyson	Old English	The son of Dennis. Wild, frenzied. Also a lover of wine. Also see Tennyson.
Tenzin	Tibetan/Sherpa	Protector of Dharma. A boy or girl's name.
Tenzing	Tibetan/Sherpa	Protector of Dharma. A boy or girl's name.
Teodor	Greek	The gift of God.
Tercan	Turkish	
Terence	Latin	Tender, good gracious.
Terje	Norse	Of Thor's spear.
Terrel	Old English	thunderer
Terrence		Tender, good gracious.
Terrie	Latin	Smooth and polished.
Terro		
Terry	Greek/Latin	Greek: The harvester or reaper. Latin: Smooth and polished. A boy or girl's name.
Tetony	Hungarian	chieftain
Teulyddog	Welsh	
Tewdwr	Welsh	
Tex	American	From Texas.
Tezer	Turkish	
Thabit	Arabic	
Thaddeaus	Latin	Courageous, praise.
Thaddeus	Greek	Gift of God.

Thai	Vietnamese	many, multiple
Thaliard		From Shakespeare's play Pericles.
Thaman	Hindu	Name of a god.
Than	Burmese	A million. An auspicious number name.
Thane	Old English	A land-holding soldier. Also a Scottish clan chieftain.
Thanos	Greek	Noble.
Thatcher	Old English	Roof fixer.
Theobald	Teutonic	A bold leader of the people.
Theobold	Old German	Boldest.
Theodore	Greek	Divine gift.
Theodoric	Teutonic	The ruler of the people. Also see Derek.
Theon	Greek	Godly.
Theophilus	Greek	Beloved of God.
Theron	Greek	The hunter.
Thersites		From Shakespeare's play Troilus & Cressida.
Theseus	Greek	A hero of Greek legend.
Thibaud	Old French	
Thidias		From Shakespeare's play Antony & Cleopatra.
Thierry	French	French form of Terence and Theodoric.
Thies	Dutch	Dutch diminutives of Matthew.
Thijs	Dutch	Dutch diminutives of Matthew.
Thomas	Greek	A twin.
Thor	Old Norse	The God of thunder in Norse mythology.
Thorald	Old Norse	Ruling in the manner of Thor.
Thoralf	Scandinavian	
Thorbjorn	Scandinavian	
Thorburn	Old Norse	Thor's warrior.
Thord	Scandinavian	
Thore	Scandinavian	

Thorfinn	Scandinavian	
Thorgeirr	Scandinavian	
Thorgils	Scandinavian, Anglo-Saxon	
Thorgrim	Scandinavian	
Thorkell	Scandinavian	
Thorleifr	Scandinavian	
Thormund	Old English	Thor's protection.
Thorne	Old English	Thorn tree.
Thornley	Old English	From the thorny clearing.
Thornton	Old English	From the place among the thorns.
Thorpe	Old English	From the farm village.
Thorstein	Scandinavian	
Thorulffr	Scandinavian	
Thorvald	Scandinavian	
Thorvid	Scandinavian	
Thosa	Old French	
Thrandr	Scandinavian	
Thurborn	Teutonic	Dweller by Thor's stream.
Thurio		From Shakespeare's play Two Gentlemen of Verona.
Thurlow	Old English	from Thor
Thurso	Scottish	A Scottish location.
Thurstan	Old English	Thor's stone.
Thurston	Norse	Thor's stone
Tibald	Teutonic	A bold leader of the people.
Tibalt	Greek	People's prince.
Tiberius	Latin	After the River Tiber.
Tibold	German	A bold leader of the people.
Tiernan	Irish Gaelic	The descendant of a lord.
Tierney	Irish Gaelic	The descendant of a lord. A boy or girl's name.
Tihamar	Hungarian	Enjoys silence.
Tiki	Polynesian	One who is fetched, as in a spirit after death.
Tilak	Hindu	

Tilford	Old English	From the good man's ford.
Tim	Greek	Honoring God, or honored by God.
Timeus	Greek	Perfect.
Timoleon	Greek	I honor what I say.
Timon	Greek	A reward, an honor. Also from Shakespeare's play Timon of Athens.
Timor		After the Timor Sea.
Timothy	Greek	Honoring God, or honored by God.
Timur	Hebrew, Hungarian, Turkish	Iron.
Tinh	Vietnamese	Mindful, aware.
Tipene	Maori	Maori form of Stephen.
Titus	Latin	An old Roman name.
Titusz	Hungarian	Dove, honored.
Tivadar	Hungarian	Gift of God.
Tivon	Hebrew	lover of nature
Tobias	Hebrew	God is good. A Biblical name.
Tobie	Hebrew	God is good. A boy or girl's name.
Toby	Hebrew	The Lord is good.
Tod		A fox or fox hunter.
Todd	Old Norse from Latin	A fox or fox hunter.
Toft	Old English	From the site of the building.
Toker	Turkish	
Tolga	Turkish	
Tom	Greek	A twin. A form of Thomas.
Tomaj	Hungarian	Name of a clan.
Tomas	Czech/Irish/Scottish Gaelic/Spanish	A twin. A form of Thomas.
Tomasz	Polish	A twin. A form of Thomas.
Tome	Galician	
Tomi	Japanese	Red.
Tomkin	Old English	Little Tom or Thomas.
Tommy	Greek	A twin. A form of Thomas.
Tomo	Greek	A twin. A form of Thomas.
Tong	Vietnamese	Fragrant.

Tony	Latin	Praiseworthy, of inestimable worth.
Tor	Old Norse/Celtic	Old Norse: The God of thunder in Norse mythology. Celtic: A rock.
Tore	Old Norse	The God of thunder in Norse mythology.
Torin	Gaelic	The chief.
Tormey	Irish Gaelic	A thunder spirit.
Tormod	Scottish	
Torquil	Scottish Gaelic from Old Norse	Thor's cauldron.
Torr	Old English	From the tower.
Torrance	Latin	Smooth and polished.
Torsten	German	Little Tom or Thomas.
Torvald	Old Norse	Thor the ruler.
Toste	Scandinavian	
Tostig	Anglo-Saxon, Scandinavian	
Touchstone		From Shakespeare's play As You Like It.
Toussaint	French	All the saints. Also see Santos.
Tovi	Modern Hebrew	Good.
Townley	Old English	From the town meadow.
Townsend	Old English	From the towns end.
Toyo	Japanese	Plentiful.
Tracy	Old French	Brave. A boy or girl's name.
Trahaearn	Welsh	Strong as iron.
Traherne	Welsh	Of iron strength.
Tran	Vietnamese	A family name.
Tranio		From Shakespeare's play Taming of the Shrew.
Tranter	Old English	Wagoneer.
Travis	Old French	From the crossing or crossroads.
Trefor	Welsh	From the large village.
Trefusis	Cornish	A location.
Trelawney	Cornish	From the church village.
Tremayne	Cornish	From the place of the stone or rock.

Tremeur	Old French	Large village
Trent	English	Thrifty. From the name of a river.
Trenus	Latin	
Tresco	Cornish	From a location, one of the Isles of Scilly.
Trethowan	Cornish	From the farm by the sandhills.
Trevelyan	Cornish	From the farm at the mill. A Cornish location.
Trevor	Welsh	Prudent. From the large village.
Trey	Middle English	Third born, three.
Trigve	Norwegian	
Trilby	Italian	Sings with trills. A boy or girl's name.
Trinculo		From Shakespeare's play The Tempest.
Trinity	Latin	A trio or triad, as in the Holy Trinity. A boy or girl's name.
Tripp	Old English	Traveler.
Trisanu	Hindu	
Tristan	Celtic	The noisy one.
Tristen	Celtic	The noisy one.
Tristram	Celtic	Sad.
Troilus	French	Name of a location.
Trowbridge	Old English	From the wooden bridge.
Troy	Old French	Water or foot soldier. From a location. Also the name of the ancient city in Asia Minor.
Truman	Old English	A trusty or faithful man.
Tryggvi	Scandinavian	
Trystan	Cornish/Welsh	The noisy one.
Tuart	Aboriginal	A type of Eucalyptus.
Tuathal	Celtic	
Tubal		From Shakespeare's play Merchant of Venice.
Tucker	Old English	A cloth-worker.
Tudfwlch	Welsh	
Tudi	Old French	

Tudor	Welsh	Welsh form of Theodore. Divine gift.
Tudur	Welsh	
Tugdual	Old French	
Tujan	Old French	
Tuncer	Turkish	
Tungyr	Welsh	
Ture	Scandinavian	
Turi	Polynesian	The name of a famous chief.
Turiau	Old French	
Turner	Old French	A lathe-worker.
Turpin	Old Norse	A Finnish man of Thor.
Tushar	Hindu	
Tuvya	Hebrew	
Tuyen	Vietnamese	Angelic.
Twain	Middle English	Two pieces.
Twyford	Old English	From the double ford.
Tyack	Cornish	A farmer.
Tybalt	Teutonic	A bold leader of the people.
Tycho	Greek	He who hits the mark.
Tye	Old English	From the enclosure.
Tyee	Native American	Chief.
Tyler	Old English	A tiler or tile-maker. A boy or girl's name.
Tymon	Greek	A reward, an honor.
Tynan	Gaelic	The dark one.
Tyne		The name of an English river. A boy or girl's name.
Tyrek		Variant of Ty.
Tyrol		After the Austrian alpine region.
Tyrone	Irish	The name of a county in Northern Ireland.
Tyrus	Latin	Person from Tyre.
Tyson	Old French	A firebrand.
Tytus	Polish	An old Roman name.
Tzuriel	Hebrew	

Uba	African	Wealthy.
Ubul	Hungarian	
Udeh	Hebrew	Praise.
Udell	Anglosaxon	From the valley of the Yew trees.
Udit	Hindu	
Udo	German	Prosperity, fortune.
Udolf	Old English	A prosperous wolf.
Uehudah	Hebrew	
Ufuk	Turkish	
Ugo	Italian	Italian form of Hugh. Heart and mind.
Ugod	Hungarian	Name of a clan.
Ugor	Hungarian	Hungarian.
Ugur	Turkish	
Uilleam	Scottish Gaelic	Scottish Gaelic form of William. A strong and resolute protector.
Uisdean	Scottish	
Uland	Teutonic	The noble land.
Ulbrecht	Teutonic	Noble splendor.
Ulf	Swedish	Wolf-like, courageous.
Ulffr	Scandinavian	
Ulfred	Old English/Teutonic	Peace.
Ulmer	Old English	A famous wolf.
Ulprus	Latin	
Ulrich	Teutonic	A ruler.
Ultan	Irish	From an old Gaelic name.
Ulucan	Turkish	
Ulysses	Greek	The angry one, wrathful. The famous wanderer of Homer's odyssey.
Umar	Arabic	Flourishing, long-lived.
Umberto	Italian	A famous warrior.
Unai	Basque	
Unni	Norse	Modest.
Unwin	Old English	The enemy.
Upen	Hindu	
Upendra	Hindu	An element.

Upor	Hungarian	
Upravda	Slavonic	The upright one.
Upton	Old English	From the upper farm or town.
Upwood	Old English	From the forest on the hill.
Urban	Latin	A city dweller. The name of several early saints and popes.
Uren	Welsh	
Uri	Russian	God is light. Also see Uriel.
Uriah	Russian	God is light. A Biblical name.
Urie	Russian	God is light. Also see Uriel.
Uriel	Hebrew	Light. Also see Uriah.
Urien	Welsh	Have privileged birth, or born in the town.
Urjavaha	Hindu	Of the Nimi dynasty.
Uros	Hungarian	Little lord.
Ursel	Latin	A bear. The masculine version of Ursula.
Urson	Old French from Latin	A little bear.
Urvan	Latin	A city dweller.
Usamah	Arabic	
Ushnisha	Sanskrit	A crown.
Usko	Finnish	Faith.
Usman	Arabic	An Ottoman Turk, or a servant of God.
Utah		The name of an American State. A boy or girl's name.
Utt	Arabic	Wise and kind.
Uttam	Hindu	Third Manu.
Uttanka	Hindu	
Utz	Teutonic	A ruler.
Uwain	Welsh	
Uwan	Aboriginal	To meet.
Uwe	Scandinavian	A well-known Scandinavian name.
Uxio	Galician	
Uyeda	Japanese	From the Rice field.

Uzi	Hebrew	My strength.
Uzor	Hungarian	Name of an ethnic group.
Uzziah	Hebrew	The power or strength of God.
Vachel	Old French	A little cow or one who raises cows.
Vaclav	Czech	Czech form of Wenceslas.
Vadim	Russian	A powerful ruler.
Vahe	Armenian	Victor.
Vaibhav	Hindu	
Vail	Old English	From the valley.
Vairaja	Hindu	Son of Virat.
Valdemar	Slavonic	A powerful ruler.
Valentin	Danish/French/Swedish	Strong, healthy.
Valentine	Latin	Strong, healthy. The name of a third century saint. A boy or girl's name.
Valentino	Italian	Strong, healthy.
Valeray	Old French, Latin	Valor, strong.
Valerian	Latin	Strong and powerful.
Vallis	Old French	The Welshman.
Valter	Teutonic	A mighty ruler.
Vamana	Sanskrit	Deserving praise.
Van	Dutch	Generally a prefix to a surname, but also used as a first name. Also from the name Ivan.
Vance	Old English	A thresher.
Vane	Old English	From the marsh or fen.
Vaninadh	Hindu	Husband of Saraswati (the goddess of knowledge).
Vanya	Russian	Eastern European form of John. From the name Ivan.
Varad	Hungarian	From the fortress.
Varden	Old French	From the green hills.
Varian	Latin	The changeable one.
Varick	Icelandic/Teutonic	Icelandic: A sea drifter. Teutonic: A protecting ruler.
Variya	Hindu	Excellent one.

Varkony	Hungarian	Name of an Avar ethnic group.
Varocher	French	
Varrius		From Shakespeare's play Measure for Measure.
Varsony	Hungarian	Name of an ethnic group.
Vartan	Armenian	A rose.
Varun	Hindu	Lord of the waters.
Varuna	Sanskrit	The God of the night sky.
Vasant	Hindu	
Vasava	Hindu	Indra
Vasilios	Greek	With royal blood, regal.
Vasily	Russian	Royal, kingly.
Vasu	Hindu	
Vasudev	Hindu	
Vasudeva	Sanskrit	The father of the God Krishna.
Vasuman	Hindu	born of fire
Vaughan	Welsh	Small.
Vavrin	Czech	Laurel.
Vavrinec	Czech	Lawrence
Vayk	Hungarian	Rich.
Vazsony	Hungarian	
Vedanga	Hindu	Vedas.
Vedmundr	Scandinavian	
Veer	Hindu	
Veit	Dutch	Dutch form of Guy.
Vekoslav	Slavonic	Eternal glory.
Vencel	Slavic	Wreath, glory.
Vencentio	Italian	Conqueror, victor.
Venec	Breton	
Venn	Old English	From the marsh or fen.
Ventidius		From Shakespeare's play Timon of Athens and Antony & Cleopatra.
Vere	Latin	Faithful and loyal.
Vered	Hebrew	A rose.

Verges		From Shakespeare's play Much Ado About Nothing.
Verner	Latin/Scandinavian	Latin: Springlike. Scandinavian: The protecting army or warrior.
Vernon	Latin	Springlike, youthful.
Verrell	French	Honest.
Viau	Breton	Lively.
Victor	Latin	Winner, conqueror. Also see Vincent.
Vid	German	Sylvan man.
Vidal	Latin	Vital, lively. Also see Vitus and Vivian.
Vidor	Hungarian	Cheerful.
Vidvan	Hindu	Scholar.
Vidya	Sanskrit	Knowledge. A boy or girl's name.
Vijay	Sanskrit	Strong and victorious.
Vikas	Hindu	Progress.
Vikram	Hindu	Glorious king.
Vikrant	Hindu	
Viktor	Czech/German/Polish/Scandinavian	The conqueror. Also see Vincent.
Vilem	Czech	A strong and resolute protector.
Vilhehn	Scandinavian	A strong and resolute protector.
Viljalmr	Scandinavian	
Vilmos	Hungarian	A strong and resolute protector.
Vimal	Sanskrit	Pure.
Vinay	Hindu	Good behavior.
Vince	Latin	Conqueror, victor.
Vincent	Latin	Conqueror, victor.
Vincentio	Italian	Conqueror, victor.
Vineet	Hindu	
Vinnie	Latin	Conqueror, victor.
Vinny	Latin	Conqueror, victor.
Vinod	Hindu	
Vinson	Latin	Conqueror, victor.
Vipin	Hindu	
Vipul	Hindu	

Viraj	Hindu	
Virasana	Hindu	
Virat	Hindu	Supreme being.
Virgil	Latin	Strong.
Visant	Breton	
Vishal	Hindu	
Vishnu	Sanskrit	The protector. An important Hindu God.
Visvajit	Hindu	One who conquers the universe.
Visvakarman	Hindu	Architect, son of Yogasiddha.
Visvayu	Hindu	Brother of Amavasuand Satayu.
Viswanath	Hindu	
Vitale	Latin	Lively. Also see Vitus and Vivian.
Vitoz	Hungarian	Brave warrior.
Vito	Latin	Conqueror.
Vittore	Italian	The conqueror. Also see Vincent.
Vittorio	Spanish	The conqueror. Also see Vincent.
Vitus	Latin	Life. The name of a Sicilian child saint. Also see Vitale and Vivian.
Vivatma	Hindu	Universal soul.
Vivek	Hindu	
Vivian	Latin	Gracious in life or lively. A boy or girl's name.
Vladilen	Russian	
Vladimir	Slavonic	Prince. A powerful ruler.
Vladislav	Slavonic	A glorious ruler. Also see Ladislav.
Volf	Jewish	Jewish form of Wolfe. .
Volker	German	
Volney	Teutonic	Of the people.
Voltimand		From Shakespeare's play Hamlet.
Vortigern	Celtic	A great king.
Voteporix	Latin	
Vougay	Breton	
Vyasa	Sanskrit	The arranger.
Vyvyan	Cornish	From an old surname. A boy or girl's name.

Wade	Old English	A wanderer, or from the river crossing.
Wagner	Dutch	A wagon driver or wagon-maker.
Wahib	Arabic	The generous one.
Wahnond	Teutonic	The mighty protector.
Wain	Old English	A cart or wagon-maker.
Waine	Old English	A cart or wagon-maker.
Wainwright	Old English	A cart or wagon-maker.
Waite	Old English	A watchman or guard.
Wakefield	Old English	Wet field.
Wakeman	Old English	A watchman.
Walby	Old Norse/Old English	The farm by the ancient wall.
Walchelim	Anglo-Norman	
Waldemar	Dutch/German/Scandinavian	A powerful ruler.
Walden	Old English	From the valley in the forest.
Waldo	Teutonic	The ruler.
Walenty	Polish	Strong, healthy.
Waleran	Anglo-Norman	
Walford	Old English	From the ford over the stream.
Walid	Arabic	The newborn boy.
Walker	Old English	A fuller. One who thickens cloth.
Wallace	Old French	A foreigner, particularly a Welshman.
Walmer	Old English	The pool of the Welsh.
Walpole	Old English	From the pool by the ancient wall.
Walsh	Old French	A foreigner, particularly a Welshman.
Walter	Teutonic	An army general.
Walton	Old English	From the farm or town of the foreigners.
Walwyn	Old English	A powerful friend.
Waman	Hindu	
Wang	Chinese	Kingly.
Warburton	Old English	From the fortress town.
Ward	Old English	A guard or watchman.
Wardell	Old English	From the valley of the River Wear.

Warfield	Old English	The field by the stream.
Warley	Old English	From the cattle pasture.
Warmund	Old English	A loyal protector.
Warner	Teutonic	The protecting army or warrior.
Warra	Aboriginal	Water.
Warrain	Aboriginal	Belonging to the sea.
Warren	Old French/Old English	To preserve. The park keeper.
Warrigal	Aboriginal	Wild, or a dingo.
Warrun	Aboriginal	The sky.
Warton	Old English	A lookout point.
Warwick	Old English	From the dairy farm at the weir. An English location.
Waseem	Arabic	
Washington	Old English	Town of the smart.
Wasim	Arabic	The handsome one.
Wassily	Sanskrit	The God of the night sky.
Watkin	Old English	The son of Walter. Or an army general.
Watson	Old English	Son of Walter.
Waverley	Old English	To wave. From the village of the Aspen trees.
Waverly	Old English	From the tree-lined meadow.
Wayde	Old English	Angel from God.
Wayland	Old English	From the land by the crossroads or roadway.
Wayne	Old English	A cart or wagon-maker. Actor John Wayne helped to make this popular as a first name.
Webb	Old English	A weaver.
Webster	Old English	A weaver.
Welby	Old Norse/Old English	From the farm by the spring.
Welch	Old French	A foreigner, particularly a Welshman.
Welcome	English	Welcome guest.
Weldon	Old English	From the hill with a spring.

Welford	Old English	From the ford by the willows.
Wellington	Old English	From the rich man's farm.
Wells	Old English	From the spring or well.
Welsh	Old French	A foreigner, particularly a Welshman.
Wen	Chinese	Cultured, or ornamental.
Wenceslas	Slavonic	Great glory. A 10th-century bohemian saint.
Wendell	Teutonic	Valley or wanderer.
Wendron	Cornish	A location.
Wenlock	Old Welsh	From the holy monastery.
Wentworth	Old English	Estate of the white-haired one, or a winter estate.
Werner	Teutonic	Warin warrior
Wesley	Old English	The West meadow.
West	Old English	A direction.
Weston	Old English	From the Western farm or town.
Westwood	Old English	From the wood to the west.
Wetherby	Old English	From the sheep farm.
Weylin	Celtic	The son of the wolf.
Weymouth	Old English	The mouth of the River Wey.
Wheatley	Old English	From the wheat meadow.
Wheaton	Old English	Wheat town.
Wheeler	Old English	A wheel-maker.
Whetu	Polynesian	A star.
Whit	Old English	White.
Whitby	Old English	The white town.
Whitcombe	Old English	From the wide valley.
Whitfield	Old English	The white field.
Whitford	Old English	From the white ford.
Whitley	Old English	The white meadow or clearing.
Whitmore	Old English	From the white moor.
Whitney	Old English	From the white island. A boy or girl's name.
Whittaker	Old English	The white field.
Wickham	Old English	From the meadow homestead.

Wid	Welsh	
Wieslav	Slavic	One with great glory.
Wihtred	Anglo-Saxon	
Wilbur	Old English	The resolute one.
Wiley	Old English	Wily or beguiling.
Wilford	Old English	The ford in the willows.
Wilfred	Teutonic	Desirous of peace. A peacemaker.
Wilkes	Old English	A strong and resolute protector.
Wilkie	Old English	A strong and resolute protector.
Will		From the name William, but sometimes used as an independent name.
Willard	Old English	Resolute and brave.
William	Teutonic	A strong and resolute protector.
Willis	Old English	A strong and resolute protector.
Willoughby	Old Norse/Old English	From the farm by the willows.
Wilmer	Teutonic	Famously resolute. From a similar origin to that of William.
Wilmot	Teutonic	Of resolute mind. Originally from the name William.
Wilson	Old English from Teutonic	The son of William. A strong and resolute protector.
Wilton	Old English	From the farm by the stream.
Wim	Dutch/German	A strong and resolute protector.
Winchester	Old English	Roman site.
Windsor	Old English	From the river bank or landing place.
Winog	Breton	
Winslow	Old English	Hill of victory.
Winston	Old English	Victory town.
Winter	Old English	Born in the winter months. A boy or girl's name.
Winthrop	Old English	From a friend's village.
Winton	Old English	From a friend's farm.
Wirrin	Aboriginal	A tea-tree.
Wistan	Old English	The battle stone.

Witton	Old English	A farm by the wood.
Wolf	English	Wolf.
Wolfe	Teutonic	Wolf-like, courageous.
Wolfgang	Teutonic	Path of a wolf.
Wolfram	Teutonic	The wolf raven.
Wolter	Dutch	Dutch form of Walter.
Woodburn	Old English	From the stream in the wood.
Woodley	Old English	The meadow or clearing in the forest.
Woodrow	Old English	The path through the woods.
Woodward	Old English	A forester, a forest guardian.
Woody		The path through the woods.
Woorak	Aboriginal	From the plain.
Woorin	Aboriginal	The sun.
Worcester	Old English	Roman site. An English city.
Wren	Old English	A tiny bird. A boy or girl's name.
Wright	Old English	A carpenter or craftsman.
Wulfhere	Anglo-Saxon	
Wulfnoth	Anglo-Saxon	
Wyatt	Teutonic	The wide one, or from the wood or water.
Wyber	Old English	A battle fortress.
Wyburn	Old English	A battle hero.
Wye	Teutonic	The wide one, or from the wood.
Wykeham	Old English	From the meadow homestead.
Wylie	Old English	Wily or beguiling. A boy or girl's name.
Wyman	Old English	A warrior.
Wyndam	Old English	The field with the winding path.
Wyndham	Old English	From the battle protector's homestead.
Wynford	Welsh	From the white ford.
Wynn	Welsh	The fair or blessed one.
Wynston	Old English	From a friend's estate or town.
Wynton	Old English	From a friend's farm.
Wyome	Native American	Plain.

Wystan	Old English	The battle stone.
Xander	Greek	Defending men. Form of Alexander
Xan	Galician	
Xanthus	Greek	Golden-haired.
Xanti	Basque	
Xavier	Arabic/Spanish	Arabic: Bright. Spanish: Of the new house.
Xenophon	Greek	Strange voices, or strong sounding.
Xenos	Greek	A stranger.
Xerxes	Persian	A king or ruler. The name of a famous Persian king.
Xiao	Galician	
Ximen	Spanish	Spanish form of Simon. The listener.
Ximenes	Spanish	Spanish form of Simon. The listener.
Ximens	Spanish	Spanish form of Simon. The listener.
Ximun	Basque	Basque form of Simon.
Xurxo	Galician	
Xylon	Basque	Basque form of Simon.
Yadon	Hebrew	He will judge.
Yael	Hebrew	A wild goat. A boy or girl's name.
Yahto	Native American	Blue.
Yakecan	Dene Indian	Sky, song.
Yakov		The modern Jewish and Russian form of Jacob. Held by the heel.
Yale	Old English/Teutonic	Old English: From the corner of the land. Teutonic: The one who pays.
Yan	Hebrew	God's grace.
Yancy	Native American	The Englishman. The word later became `Yankee'.
Yanis	Hebrew	God's gift
Yannick	French	
Yannis	Greek	Greek form of John.
Yaphet	Hebrew	Youthful.
Yardley	Old English	From the enclosed meadow.
Yarin	Hebrew	To understand.
Yarn	Breton	Form of John.

Yarran	Aboriginal	An Acacia tree.
Yasar	Arabic	
Yash	Hindu	
Yashodhar	Hindu	
Yashovarman	Hindu	
Yashpal	Hindu	
Yasir	Arabic	Wealthy.
Yasuo	Japanese	Peaceful one.
Yates	Middle English	The keeper of the gates.
Yazid	Arabic	Ever increasing.
Yefrem	Russian	Fruitful. One of the sons of Joseph in the Bible.
Yehuda	Jewish	The praised one.
Yehudi	Hebrew	Praise to the Lord or a person from Judah. A boy or girl's name.
Yener	Turkish	
Yered	Hebrew	Form of Jared.
Yerik	Russian	appointed by God
Yervant	Armenian	an Armenian king
Yeshaya	Hebrew	
Yeshe	Tibetan/Sherpa	Wise one.
Yestin	Welsh	Welsh form of Justin. Just or true.
Yevgeni	Russian	The noble, well-born one.
Yigael	Hebrew	God will redeem.
Yigit	Turkish	
Yileen	Aboriginal	A dream.
Yitzaak	Hebrew	Laughter, the laughing one.
Yitzak	Hebrew	Laughter, the laughing one.
Yngvar	Norse	Of the army.
Ynyr	Welsh	Honor.
Yobachi	African	Pray to God.
Yoel	Hebrew	The Lord is God.
Yogendra	Hindu	
Yogesh	Hindu	
Yogi	Japanese	One of the yoga practice.

Yona	Hebrew/Native American	Hebrew: A dove. Native American: A bear. A boy or girl's name.
Yong	Korean	The brave one.
Yoram	Hebrew	The Lord is exalted.
Yorick	Greek	A tiller of the soil (farmer). From the name George.
York	Celtic/Old English	Celtic: The farm of the Yew tree. Old English: A boar farm.
Yosef	Hebrew	God shall add.
Yoshifumi	Japanese	
Yoshimitsu	Japanese	
Yoshiyuki	Japanese	
Ysgarran	Welsh	
Yuan	Chinese	The original.
Yudhajit	Hindu	
Yuka	Aboriginal	A tree.
Yukio	Japanese	Gets what he wants, God will nourish.
Yul	Latin	A Roman family name, possibly meaning youthful. Born in July.
Yule	Old English	Born at Christmas.
Yuma	Native American	The son of a chief.
Yuri	Aboriginal/Japanese/Russian	Aboriginal: To hear. Also the Russian form of George. A boy or girl's name.
Yusuf	Arabic	Arabic form of Joseph.
Yutaka	Japanese	
Yves	French	The little archer.
Zabulon	Hebrew	To exalt, honor.
Zaccheo	Hebrew	The one God remembers.
Zachariah		Remembered by the Lord.
Zacharias		Remembered by the Lord.
Zachary	Hebrew	The Lord has remembered.
Zadok	Hebrew	Just, righteous.
Zador	Hungarian	Violent.
Zafar	Arabic	The triumphant one.
Zafer	Turkish	
Zagger	unknown	

Zagon	Hungarian	
Zahin	Hindu	
Zahir	Arabic	Shining, radiant.
Zahneny	Hebrew	Wise and peaceful.
Zahur	Egyptian	A flower.
Zaid	African	Increase, growth.
Zaide	Yiddish	Elder.
Zajzon	Hungarian	
Zakai	Aramaic, Hebrew	Innocent, one who is pure.
Zaki	Arabic	Pure.
Zalen	Hungarian	thrower, hitter
Zale	Old English	To sell, or a salary.
Zalman	Yiddish	Wise and peaceful.
Zamir	Hebrew	A songbird.
Zamor	Hungarian	Plow land.
Zander	Greek	The protector and helper of mankind. Also see Sanders.
Zane	Hebrew	God is gracious. A boy or girl's name.
Zanebono	Italian	The good one.
Zani	Albanian	
Zaniel	Latin	Angel of Mondays
Zanipolo	Italian	Little gift of God.
Zann	Hebrew	
Zanobi	Latin	Scarcely alive.
Zarend	Hungarian	Gold.
Zared	Hebrew	An ambush.
Zarek	Greek	May God protect the king.
Zavier	Arabic/Spanish	Arabic: Bright. Spanish: Of the new house.
Zayden	Hebrew	
Zazu	Hebrew	Movement.
Zbigniew	Slavonic	To get rid of anger. A common Polish name.
Zdenek	Czech	One from Sidon, a winding sheet.
Zebadiah	Hebrew	Gift of the Lord.

Zebedeo	Aramaic	Servant of God.
Zebulon	Hebrew	Home.
Zebulun	Hebrew	Exaltation or the dwelling place. One of the sons of Leah and Jacob in the Bible.
Zechariah	Hebrew	The Lord has remembered.
Zedekiah	Hebrew	The justice of the Lord.
Zeeman	Dutch	A sailor or seaman.
Zefirino	Greek	Wind of Spring.
Zeke	Hebrew	God strengthens, or the strength of God. From the name Ezekiel.
Zeki	Turkish	
Zeko	Hungarian	
Zelig	Jewish	Blessed fortunate.
Zelipe	Aragonese	
Zelman	Hebrew	Wise and peaceful.
Zelotes	Greek	Zealous.
Zenas	Greek	Living.
Zennor	Cornish	The name of a village. A boy or girl's name.
Zeno	Greek	A stranger.
Zenoa	Hebrew	
Zenobio	Greek	Strength of Jupiter.
Zenon	Greek	A stranger.
Zenos	Greek	A stranger.
Zephan	Hebrew	Treasured by God.
Zephaniah	Hebrew	Hidden by God.
Zeren	Turkish	
Zerind	Hungarian	Serb.
Zero	Greek	Seeds.
Zeroun	Armenian	A sage.
Zetany	Hungarian	
Zeth	Greek	Investigator, researcher.
Zeus	Greek	The father of the Gods, or living. The ruler of the heavens in ancient Greek mythology.

Zev	Hebrew, Hindu	Deer, wolf.
Zia	Arabic	Splendor or ripened grain. A boy or girl's name.
Ziff	Hebrew	Wolf.
Ziggy	Slavonic	To get rid of anger. A common Polish name.
Zigmond	Teutonic	A victorious protector.
Zigmund	Teutonic	A victorious protector.
Zion	Hebrew	A sign.
Zircon	Persian	A mineral name.
Ziv	Hebrew	Full of life.
Ziven	Slavic	Vigorous and alive.
Zoard	Hungarian	
Zobor	Hungarian	Gathering.
Zoello	Greek	Son of Zoe.
Zoilo	Greek	Lively.
Zoland	Hebrew	
Zoltan	Arabic	A ruler or sultan. A popular Hungarian name.
Zombor	Hungarian	Buffalo.
Zoran	Slavonic	Of the dawn.
Zoroaster	Persian	A golden star.
Zorro	Slavic	Golden dawn.
Zosimo	Greek	Lively.
Zotico	Greek	Lively.
Zowie	Gaelic	
Zsigmond	Hungairan	Victorious defender.
Zsolt	Hungarian	Name of an honor.
Zubin	Hebrew	The exalted one.
Zuriel	Hebrew	God is my foundation.
Zurl	Hebrew	